# The Psyche on Stage

Marie-Louise von Franz, Honorary Patron

**Studies in Jungian Psychology
by Jungian Analysts**

Daryl Sharp, General Editor

# The Psyche on Stage
## Individuation Motifs in Shakespeare and Sophocles

*Measure for Measure*
Wholeness Lost and Found

*Romeo and Juliet*
A Coniunctio Drama

*Oedipus Rex*
Mythology and the Tragic Hero

**EDWARD F. EDINGER**
Edited with Forewords by Sheila Dickman Zarrow

Edward F. Edinger is the author of 13 other books in this Series.
*See page 94 for details.*

**Canadian Cataloguing in Publication Data**

Edinger, Edward F. (Edward Ferdinand), 1922-
  The psyche on stage: individuation motifs in Shakespeare and Sophocles

(Studies in Jungian psychology by Jungian analysts; 93)

Contents: Measure for measure: wholeness lost and found—
Romeo and Juliet: a coniunctio drama—
Oedipus Rex: mythology and the tragic hero.

Includes bibliographical references and index.

ISBN 0-919123-94-5

1. Shakespeare, William, 1564-1616—Knowledge—Psychology.
2. Jung, C.G. (Carl Gustav), 1875-1961—Views on literature.
3. Shakespeare, William, 1564-1616. Measure for measure.
4. Shakespeare, William, 1564-1616. Romeo and Juliet.
5. Sophocles. Oedipus Rex. 6. Archetype (Psychology) in literature.
7. Psychoanalysis and literature. 8. Drama—psychological aspects.
I. Zarrow, Sheila Dickman, 1952-. II. Title. III. Series.

PR3065.E33 2001    822.3'3    C00-931768-6

Copyright © 2001 by Dianne C. Cordic. All rights reserved.

INNER CITY BOOKS
Box 1271, Station Q, Toronto, ON M4T 2P4, Canada

Telephone (416) 927-0355 / FAX (416) 924-1814
Web site: www.innercitybooks.net / E-mail: info@innercitybooks.net

Honorary Patron: Marie-Louise von Franz.
Publisher and General Editor: Daryl Sharp.
Senior Editor: Victoria Cowan.

INNER CITY BOOKS was founded in 1980 to promote the
understanding and practical application of the work of C.G. Jung.

Index by Victoria Cowan.

Printed and bound in Canada by University of Toronto Press Incorporated

# CONTENTS

Acknowledgments and Illustrations   7

*Edward F. Edinger*   8

*Measure for Measure:* **Wholeness Lost and Found**   9
Foreword   11
   Introduction   13
   A Summary of the Story   15
   A Psychological Study of the Play   17
   Concluding Remarks   32

*Romeo and Juliet:* **A Coniunctio Drama**   43
Foreword   45
   Introduction   47
   A Psychological Study of the Play   49
   Concluding Remarks   65

*Oedipus Rex:* **Mythology and the Tragic Hero**   67
Foreword   69
   Introduction   71
   The Tragic Hero   72
   The Psyche on Stage   74
   Oedipus the King   77
   Oedipus at Colonus   83

Bibliography   87

Index   90

*See final pages for other Inner City Books*

# Acknowledgments

*Measure for Measure:* **Wholeness Lost and Found** was originally a paper presented in part at the 1992 North/South Conference in Asilomar, California. It has not previously been published.

*Romeo and Juliet:* **A Coniunctio Drama** first appeared in *The Shaman from Elko: Papers in Honor of Joseph L. Henderson on His Seventy-fifth Birthday,* edited by Gareth S. Hill and published by the C.G. Jung Institute of San Francisco, 1978.

*Oedipus Rex:* **Mythology and the Tragic Hero** was originally an article in *Parabola* magazine, vol. 1, no. 1 (Winter 1976), entitled "The Tragic Hero: An Image of Individuation." Parts of it appeared as "The Tragic Drama: Oedipus," in Edward F. Edinger, *The Eternal Drama: The Inner Meanng of Greek Mythology,* published in 1994 by Shambhala Publications, Boston.

## Illustrations

*Source credits are given in the captions*

**Page**
28. The Goddess of Justice (Marseilles Tarot card).
29. The soul of the deceased being weighed in the balance.
30. The Archangel Michael weighing souls.
35. Adam Kadmon and the Sefirotic Tree.
50. Dove descending between king and queen.
57. The slaying of the king.
61. King and queen lying dead in the tomb.
64. The new birth.
79. Young Oedipus ponders the Sphinx's riddle.
84. Hexagram 56, "The Wanderer."

Edward F. Edinger, 1922-1998

## *MEASURE FOR MEASURE*
## Wholeness Lost and Found

The *imago Dei* . . . makes mankind its involuntary exponent.
—C.G. Jung, "Answer to Job."

# Foreword

In 1992, Edward F. Edinger presented a paper, "Wholeness Lost and Found: The Ego-Self Relation as Revealed in Shakespeare's *Measure for Measure,"* at the North/South Conference in Asilomar, California. Dr. Edinger prepared substantially more notes than he included in the North/South presentation. I am honored to be invited to synthesize and edit the two sets of material and present here his considered reflections on *Measure for Measure.*

Edinger asks us to consider what the figure of the Duke (psychological representation of the Self) teaches us about the nature of the Self. He guides us to the answer by means of an interesting walking tour of the play. The mystery of the nature of the Self is unfolded in comprehensive steps event by event, character by character through the basic plot.

Events are set in motion by the Duke, who delegates to Angelo (psychological representation of the ego) the task of correcting the lax behavior of the people of Vienna. Why did the Duke let things fall into a condition he did not like? And why did he take such a circuitous route to straighten things out?

Edinger answers the questions in terms of Jung's basic paradigm about why the Self needs the ego in order to achieve its desired result—restoration of the ever-present archetype of wholeness which has disappeared from the purview of consciousness. The psyche's paradoxical God-image, which needs individual consciousness for its realization, is distinguished from the conventional God-image. This distinction makes understanding Jung's psychology of the individuation process much more accessible.

The religious function of the psyche, about which much has been written but too little understood, really needed this little gem in which Edinger clearly distinguishes psychological underpinnings from customary religious or theological underpinnings.

In the preface to his book *Ego and Archetype,* Edinger writes,

> Pronouncements are not sufficient to convey new levels of consciousness. The realization of the "reality of the psyche" which makes this new world-view visible, can only be achieved by one individual at a time working laboriously on his own personal development. This individual opus is called by Jung *individuation*—a process in which the ego becomes increasingly aware of its origin from and dependence upon the archetypal psyche.[1]

"Wholeness Lost and Found" is such an enlivening illustration of the individuation process that it reminded me of an inspired poem by Rilke. I include it here as a thank you note to Dr. Edinger.

> As once the winged energy of delight
> carried you over childhood's dark abysses,
> now beyond your own life build the great
> arch of unimagined bridges.
>
> Wonders happen if we can succeed
> in passing through the harshest danger;
> but only in a bright and purely granted
> achievement can we realize the wonder.
>
> To work with Things in the indescribable
> relationship is not too hard for us;
> the pattern grows more intricate and subtle,
> and being swept along is not enough.
>
> Take your practiced powers and stretch them out
> until they span the chasm between two
> contradictions . . . For the god
> wants to know himself in you.[2]

*Sheila Dickman Zarrow*

---

[1] *Ego and Archetype,* p. xiii.
[2] "As Once the Winged Energy of Delight," in Stephen Mitchell, ed. and trans., *Ahead of All Parting: Selected Poetry and Prose of Rainer Maria Rilke,* p. 169.

# Introduction

The hallmark of Jungian psychology, that which distinguishes it decisively from all other schools of psychotherapy, is its understanding that the individual psyche has two centers of potential consciousness and will, namely, the ego and the Self. As Jung puts it, the ego is the exponent, the representative or deputy, of the Self. Thus to the extent that the ego is a carrier of authority, it derives that authority from the Self which has delegated it, so to speak. This would be the personal equivalent to the idea of divine right of kings delegated by the grace of God.

Shakespeare's play *Measure for Measure* is an interesting elaboration of the theme of delegated authority which offers us some valuable insights into the nature of the relation between ego and Self. Jung writes:

> The term "self"[3] seemed to me a suitable one for this unconscious substrate, whose actual exponent in consciousness is the ego. The ego stands to the self as the moved to the mover, or as object to subject, because the determining factors which radiate out from the self surround the ego on all sides and are therefore supraordinate to it. The self, like the unconscious, is an *a priori* existent out of which the ego evolves. It is, so to speak, an unconscious prefiguration of the ego. It is not I who create myself, rather I happen to myself. This realization is of fundamental importance for the psychology of religious phenomena.... But, fundamental as it is, it can be only half the psychological truth. If it were the whole truth it would be tantamount to determinism, for if man were merely a creature that came into being as a result of something already existing unconsciously,

---

[3] [Readers will note that the translators of Jung's *Collected Works* did not capitalize the word "self" when it refers to the archetype. In this book, as in most current Jungian writing, it is capitalized throughout in order to avoid confusion with the ego-self.—Ed.]

he would have no freedom and there would be no point in consciousness. Psychology must reckon with the fact that despite the causal nexus man does enjoy a feeling of freedom, which is identical with autonomy of consciousness. However much the ego can be proved to be dependent and preconditioned, it cannot be convinced that it has no freedom. An absolutely preformed consciousness and a totally dependent ego would be a pointless farce, since everything would proceed just as well or even better unconsciously. The existence of ego consciousness has meaning only if it is free and autonomous. By stating these facts we have, it is true, established an antinomy, but we have at the same time given a picture of things as they are. There are temporal, local, and individual differences in the degree of dependence and freedom. In reality both are always present: the supremacy of the self and the hybris of consciousness.[4]

Two additional relevant sentences at the end of the above passage, included in Jung's original essay, were omitted from its republication in the *Collected Works*. They are:

If ego consciousness follows its own road exclusively, it is trying to become like a god or a superman. But exclusive recognition of its dependence only leads to a childish fatalism and to a world-negating and misanthropic spiritual arrogance.[5]

The relation between the ego and the Self is *the* great mystery of human existence. In my view this is the basic theme of *Measure for Measure,* and we have much to learn from a psychological study of this play.

A.L. Rowse calls *Measure for Measure* "an inspired play,"[6] and I agree. It was first performed at court in December, 1604. According to the best scholarship, it had been written during the same year, and it was thus composed at about the same time as *Othello*. It followed *Hamlet* by three or four years, and preceded *King Lear* and

---

[4] "Transformation Symbolism in the Mass," *Psychology and Religion,* CW 11, par. 391. [CW refers throughout to *The Collected Works of C.G. Jung*]
[5] Julius Baum et al, eds., *The Mysteries Papers,* vol. 2, p. 324.
[6] *William Shakespeare: A Biography,* pp. 56f.

*Macbeth* by a year or so.⁷ This places it squarely among Shakespeare's most performed works.

For many commentators the play has been a chronic problem. Although it is listed among Shakespeare's comedies because it has a happy ending, all agree that its content is scarcely comic. Coleridge said of it:

> *Measure for Measure* is the single exception to the delightfulness of Shakespeare's plays. It is a hateful work, although Shakespearean throughout. Our feelings of justice are grossly wounded in Angelo's escape. Isabella herself contrives to be unamiable and Claudio is detestable.⁸

It is my thesis that the apparent problems of the play are largely resolved by considering it in the light of the ego's relation to the Self—what Jung calls the paradoxical God-image.⁹

## A Summary of the Story

Duke Vicentio, the ruler of Vienna, is concerned at the laxity of law enforcement whereby "liberty plucks justice by the nose."¹⁰ Rather than impose harsh reforms himself he decides to retire from the city for a time and delegate his authority to Angelo, a man of "unsoiled name" and austere life,¹¹ who is ordered to reform the lax behavior of the Viennese. Then the Duke, instead of visiting Poland as he had announced, disguises himself as a friar in order that he may spy on the conduct of his deputy.

Angelo's first action is to revive an old statute which imposes the death penalty for fornication. The first person to be sentenced as an example is Claudio, a young noble who has impregnated Julia,

---

⁷ R.C. Bald, ed., *The Pelican Shakespeare: Measure for Measure*, p. 14.
⁸ *Coleridge's Writings on Shakespeare*, p. 250.
⁹ "Jung and Religious Belief," *The Symbolic Life*, CW 18, par. 1681.
¹⁰ Act 1, scene 3, line 29. [Note: line numbering, spelling and punctuation may vary slightly between published versions of Shakespeare's plays.—Ed.]
¹¹ Act 1, scene 3, line 12.

his betrothed. Claudio's sister, Isabella, who is about to enter a nunnery, is asked by her brother to plead with Angelo for his life. Isabella does so very eloquently, and gradually Angelo becomes enamored of the chaste and virtuous young woman. He offers to spare Claudio's life if Isabella will give herself to him sexually. Isabella rejects this proposition vigorously, saying, "More than our brother is our chastity."[12]

The Duke, disguised as a Friar, learns of these matters and arranges a ruse. Several years previously, Angelo had rejected Mariana, his betrothed, because of an inadequate dowry. The Friar/Duke proposes that Isabella pretend to yield to Angelo and make a midnight assignation with him, then substitute in her place the wronged Mariana. This plan, the so-called bed trick, is duly executed but Angelo, fearing that his villainy will be disclosed, violates the agreement and orders the immediate execution of Claudio, demanding that Claudio's severed head be sent him. This order is thwarted by the Friar/Duke, who connives with the jail-keeper to substitute the head of another prisoner who has died a natural death.

The Duke now makes arrangements for his public return to Vienna. Angelo and other officials are to meet him at the city gate. There Isabella openly accuses Angelo of murder, hypocrisy and rape, and Mariana makes her claim to be recognized as Angelo's wife. Then the Duke reveals his prior disguise and orders that justice be done: "An Angelo for Claudio, death for death."[13] However since the order of execution was not actually carried out and with both Mariana and Isabella pleading that mercy be shown, the death penalty is revoked. Instead a multiple marriage is arranged. Claudio marries Juliet. Angelo marries Mariana, and the Duke himself sues for the hand of Isabella.[14] And so the play ends happily.

---

[12] Act 2, scene 4, line 184.
[13] Act 5, scene 1, line 407.
[14] This summary closely follows that found in Homer Watt, Karl Holzhnect, Raymond Ross, eds., *Outlines of Shakespeare's Plays,* pp. 81ff.

## A Psychological Study of the Play

From a psychological point of view, in terms of Jung's model of the psyche, the Duke represents the Self and Angelo the ego. At the beginning of the play, the initial state, the Duke is ruling his realm. This is the state of original wholeness but the condition is not satisfactory. Change is required. There then begins a dynamic relationship between ego and Self, which I shall divide into three phases.

1) In the first phase, the Duke, representing the Self, delegates his transpersonal authority to Angelo (ego), gives him an assignment, then disappears.

2) In the second phase, Angelo (ego) exercises his delegated authority and in the process identifies with it as though it were his personal possession, all the while being watched by the Duke-Self.

3) In the third phase, the missing Self reappears and there is a Day of Judgment in which the ego is held accountable.

I shall discuss each of these three phases in turn.

*1) The Self delegates its transpersonal authority to the ego and then disappears*

At the beginning of the play we learn that the Duke's realm is in a state of disorder. Laws have gone unenforced and a general state of license prevails. The Duke describes it this way:

> We have strict statutes and most biting laws,
> The needful bits and curbs to headstrong jades,
> Which for this fourteen years we have let slip;
> Even like an o'ergrown lion in a cave,
> That goes not out to prey. Now, as fond fathers,
> Having bound up the threat'ning twigs of birch,
> Only to stick it in their children's sight
> For terror, not to use, in time the rod
> Becomes more mock'd than fear'd: so our decrees,
> Dead to infliction, to themselves are dead,

> And Liberty plucks Justice by the nose,
> The baby beats the nurse, and quite athwart
> Goes all decorum.[15]

This is the state of original wholeness. Ego and Self are identified unconsciously and King baby rules.

Very interestingly, the Duke does not feel able to correct the situation himself. After hearing about the deplorable state of affairs Friar Thomas points out to the Duke,

> It rested in your Grace
> To unloose this tied-up justice when you pleas'd;
> And it in you more dreadful would have seem'd
> Than in Lord Angelo.[16]

To this the Duke replies,

> I do fear, too dreadful:
> Sith 'twas my fault to give the people scope,
> 'Twould be my tyranny to strike and gall them
> For what I bid them do: for we bid this be done,
> When evil deeds have their permissive pass,
> And not the punishment. Therefore indeed, my father,
> I have on Angelo impos'd the office;
> Who may, in th'ambush of my name strike home,
> And yet my nature never in the fight,
> To do in slander.[17]

The Self cannot correct the condition by itself. It needs the ego to do it. That is why the Duke had earlier delegated his authority to his subordinate, Angelo, asking that he be brought forward:

> For you must know, we have with special soul
> Elected him our absence to supply;
> Lent him our terror, drest him with our love,

---

[15] Act 1, scene 3, lines 19-31.
[16] Act 1, scene 3, lines 32-35.
[17] Act 1, scene 3, lines 34-43.

And given his deputation all the organs
Of our own power ...[18]

This passage announces Angelo's "election," analogous to Yahweh's election of Israel[19] and God's election of Christ.[20]

The Duke now addresses Angelo. Although Shakespeare does not have our psychological terminology he describes what we understand as the Self with complete clarity:

There is a kind of character in thy life,
That to the observer doth thy history
Fully unfold. Thyself and thy belongings
Are not thine own so proper as to waste
Thyself upon thy virtues, they on thee.
Heaven doth with us as we with torches do,
Not light them for themselves; for if our virtues
Did not go forth of us, 'twere all alike
As if we had them not ...[21]

The phrase "There is a kind of character in thy life" refers to a cipher (or sign) for secret correspondence.[22] It is an image of a transpersonal destiny that writes its signature in the personal life of the individual. Shakespeare is saying this is the source of our "virtues" and of the light that we are called upon to shine forth, not for ourselves but for the transpersonal purpose for which it is given. G. Wilson Knight[23] sees this passage as a reference to Matthew:

Ye are the light of the world, A city that is set on an hill cannot be hid,

---

[18] Act 1, scene 1, lines 17-21.
[19] Exod. 9:16: "For this cause have I raised thee up, for to shew in thee my power; and that my name may be declared throughout all the earth." (Biblical references are to the Authorized King James Version unless otherwise noted.)
[20] Matt. 3:17: "And lo a voice from heaven, saying, This is my beloved Son, in whom I am well pleased."
[21] Act 1, scene 1, lines 27-35.
[22] C.T. Onions, *A Shakespeare Glossary*, p. 36.
[23] "*Measure for Measure* and the Gospels," in Sylvan Barnet ed., *Measure for Measure*, p. 157.

Neither do men light a candle, and put it under a bushel, but on a candlestick; and it giveth light into all that are in the house.[24]

The Duke then proceeds to deputize Angelo with his (the Duke's) power:

> Hold therefore, Angelo:
> In our remove, be thou at full ourself.[25]
>
> Your scope is as mine own
> So to enforce or qualify the laws
> As to your soul seems good.[26]

What is so striking to me about the situation understood psychologically is that the Self delegates the ego to take responsibility for cleaning up the mess created by the Self's former laxness, while at the same time holding itself blameless. The ego is the one, says the Self,

> Who may, in the ambush of my name, strike home,
> And yet my nature never in the fight,
> To do it slander.[27]

Thus Angelo is set up to be the Duke's scapegoat.

At first Angelo had reacted much the same as Moses did when given his assignment by Yahweh: he protests that he is not fit for the task:

> Now, good my lord,
> Let there be some more test made of my metal
> Before so noble and so great a figure
> Be stamped upon it.[28]

This remark is rich in allusion. The pun on mettle-metal leads into the image of the coin stamped with the figure of the King

---

[24] Matt. 5:14-15.
[25] Act 1, scene 1, lines 42-43.
[26] Act 1, scene 1, lines 64-66.
[27] Act 1, scene 3, lines 41-43.
[28] Act 1, scene 3, lines 47-50.

which corresponds to the common material of the ego stamped with the archetype of the Self.[29] The reference to the testing of a metal calls to mind Yahweh's announcement to Israel:

> Behold, I have refined thee, but not with silver; I have chosen thee in the furnace of affliction.
> For mine own sake, even for mine own sake, will I do it.[30]

Angelo's remark suggests that he dimly realizes what is in store for him, namely a Job-like testing. In fact the Duke announces specifically such an intention:

> Lord Angelo is precise [i.e., Puritan],
> Stands at a guard with envy; scarce confesses
> That his blood flows, or that his appetite
> Is more to bread than stone: Hence shall we see
> If power change purpose, what our seemers be.[31]

Just as Yahweh set up Job, so Angelo is set up to be tempted out of his one-sidedness by being forced to carry the authority of the Self, the archetype of wholeness. This is the fateful issue that lies behind what we call the "power problem."

*2) The ego exercises its delegated authority and personally identifies with that authority*

In the second phase of the process, the Self has apparently disappeared, leaving the ego to exercise its delegated authority. However the hidden eye of the Self continues to operate. The Duke, disguised as a friar, keeps watch over all of Angelo's actions.

---

[29] Jung: "An archetype means a *typos* (imprint), a definite grouping of archaic character containing, in form as well as meaning, *mythological motifs.*" ("The Tavistock Lectures," *The Symbolic Life,* CW 18, par. 80) "When I say as a psychologist that God is an archetype, I mean by that the 'type' in the psyche. The word 'type' is, as we know, derived from *[typos],* 'blow' or 'imprint'; thus an archetype presupposes an imprinter." *(Psychology and Alchemy,* CW 12, par. 15)
[30] Isa. 48:10-11.
[31] Act 1, scene 3, lines 50-54.

## 22 Measure for Measure

The basic problem in the realm is an imbalance between opposites. The opposites most intensely constellated are Freedom and Discipline, Love and Law, Nature and Spirit. We are told that "Liberty plucks Justice by the nose."[32] Specifically it is erotic license that is mushrooming in Vienna, as indicated by the prominence of brothel imagery in the play. When Lucio asks Claudio, "Whence comes this restraint [on fornication]," Claudio replies,

> From too much liberty, my Lucio, Liberty:
> As surfeit, is the father of much fast;
> So every scope by the immoderate use
> Turns to restraint. Our natures do pursue,
> Like rats that ravin down their proper bane,[33]
> A thirsty evil; and when we drink, we die.[34]

In fact, all of the characters in this play are one-sided and out of balance, including the Duke and the saintly Isabella. Angelo proceeds to set matters right as he was specifically commissioned by the Duke to do. He begins with a neglected law against fornication which calls for the death penalty. Claudio, a young nobleman who has made his fiancée pregnant has been sentenced as an example of the new strict enforcement. He is imprisoned and awaits execution. Thus we see that on the same day Angelo receives the delegated authority from the Duke, he identifies with that authority and takes a fanatically one-sided position which is the opposite of the prior laxity. The wise Escalus suggests that he consult his better consciousness:

> Let but your honour know—
> Whom I believe to be most straight in virtue—
> That in the working of your own affections,
> Had time cohered with place, or place with wishing,
> Or that the resolute acting of your blood

---

[32] Act 1, scene 3, line 29.
[33] = gulp down what is poisonous to them.
[34] Act 1, scene 2, lines 116-122.

>     Could have attained th'effect of your own purpose,
>     Whether you had not sometime in your life
>     Erred on this point, which now you censure him,
>     And pulled the law upon you.[35]

This passage is a marvelous caution against shadow projection. Angelo reveals his inflation by his reply:

> 'Tis one thing to be tempted, Escalus,
> Another thing to fall.[36]

By this remark Angelo reveals that his self-righteous ego must infallibly experience a fall if his individuation is to proceed. The fall is then arranged through the agency of the anima, Isabella.

Claudio's sister, Isabella, is engaged on Claudio's behalf to sue for mercy from Angelo. Isabella, who is about to enter the nunnery, is a young woman of exemplary virtue and chastity. Lucio the braggart, "fellow of much license,"[37] says to her,

> I hold you as a thing enskied and sainted
> By your renouncement, an immortal spirit,
> And to be talked with in sincerity
> As with a saint.[38]

Isabella has a certain psychological similarity to Angelo. Both are one-sided, both destined for a fall in the course of the play, although Angelo's fall is the more obvious. Isabella proceeds to visit Angelo and pleads eloquently for her brother's life. Gradually Angelo falls under the spell of this earnest, attractive young woman.

The psychological reasons for Angelo's infatuation with Isabella are not hard to find. The opposites of Mercy and Law are constellated. Isabella is the exponent of Mercy and Angelo espouses Law. With the activation of the *coniunctio* archetype, these opposites

---

[35] Act 2, scene 1, lines 8-16.
[36] Act 2, scene 1, lines 17-18.
[37] Act 3, scene 2, line 198.
[38] Act 1, scene 4, lines 34-37.

must engage each other. The *coniunctio* archetype is a fundamental feature of the Self, so that whenever the Self is constellated so is *coniunctio,* which is the process archetype of the Self. When the activation of that archetype is decreed, so to speak, these opposites cannot go their separate ways.

As soon as the Duke left, Angelo became a fanatical upholder of the Law. This corresponds to the tendency of the immature ego to brashly assume the correctness of its judgments. Isabella urges him to mitigate the harshness of the Law with its opposite, Mercy:

> Alas, alas!
> Why are the souls that were, were forfeit once,
> And He that might the vantage best have took,
> Found out the remedy. How would you be,
> If He who is the top of judgment, should
> But judge you as you are? O, think on that,
> And mercy then will breathe within your lips,
> Like man new made.[39]

Angelo claims not to be personally identified with the law he is expending. He replies,

> Be you content, fair maid;
> It is law, not I, condemns your brother:
> Were he my kinsman, brother, or my son,
> It should be thus with him. He must die tomorrow.[40]

When asked again to show pity he makes a valid argument:

> I show it most of all when I show justice;
> For then I pity those I do not know,
> Which a dismissed offense would after gall,
> And do him right that, answering one foul wrong,
> Lives not to act another.[41]

---

[39] Act 2, scene 2, lines 72-79.
[40] Act 2, scene 2, lines 79-82.
[41] Act 2, scene 2, lines 101-105.

Like Creon in Sophocles' *Antigone*, and Captain Vere in Melville's *Billy Budd*, Angelo chooses law over mercy in this conflict of opposites. Without realizing it Angelo is caught in a profound conflict of duties. His attempt to bypass this conflict by an arbitrary choice will not stand up to psychic reality. The *coniunctio* archetype has been constellated and it demands a union of opposites. It is not Angelo's sin that he is wrong; it is his sin that he is fanatically half right.

What follows is a demonstration of the psychology of individuation and of the phenomenology of projection. *The neglected opposite ambushes Angelo from the unconscious.* He falls into an erotic transference onto Isabella and makes her a proposition: have sexual relations with him and he will spare her brother's life.

What has happened psychologically is that Angelo, the man of principle, has abandoned the principle he lives by. From the standpoint of the ego this is a moral disaster. From the standpoint of individuation the issue is less clear. Certainly the principle by which Angelo has lived has been defeated. But one principle (read archetype) can only be defeated by another which is more comprehensive and all-embracing. Seen objectively, Angelo's principle of Law has been defeated by the principle of the *coniunctio,* but since the event takes place unconsciously it manifests in a crude, inferior way as a blackmailed rape.

Nevertheless, seen as a symbolic image, the anticipated sexual union of Angelo, the proponent of Law and Isabella, the proponent of Mercy, is a *coniunctio* of Sol and Luna on the unconscious level. Such events, because they are unconscious, often have the most tragic consequences for the participants, who if they could but realize the meaning of the archetypal drama they are living out, would be rescued from the worst feature of their tragedy, namely, meaninglessness.

Angelo has fallen, a traitor to his partial principle of Law. Now it is Isabella's turn to fall. Her partial principle of Mercy will also be defeated.

*26 Measure for Measure*

Initially Isabella rejects Angelo's proposition and visits her brother in prison to inform him of the situation. As it dawns on Claudio that he really faces death he recoils from the prospect.

> Sweet sister, let me live.
> What sin you do to save a brother's life,
> Nature dispenses with the deed so far
> That it becomes a virtue.[42]

On hearing this plea, the unacknowledged opposite in Isabella erupts from the unconscious with primordial power.

> Oh you beast!
> O faithless coward, O dishonest wretch!
> Wilt thou be made a man out of my vice?
> Is't not a kind of incest, to take life
> From thine own sister's shame?[43]
>
> Take my defiance,
> Die! perish! Might but my bending down
> Reprieve thee from thy fate, it should proceed.
> I'll pray a thousand prayers for thy death;
> No word to save thee.[44]
>
> O, fie, fie, fie!
> Thy sin's not accidental, but a trade;
> Mercy to thee would prove itself a bawd,
> 'Tis best that thou diest quickly.[45]

At this high point in the onslaught of affect a miracle occurs. The Duke suddenly appears and asks for a word with Isabella. Abruptly, the affect storm terminates and the play shifts to a new level, because at this point the disguised Duke ends his passive observation and begins an active manipulation of circumstance to achieve his end. Thus Isabella's outburst is the very pivot of the play.

---

[42] Act 3, scene 1, lines 132-135.
[43] Act 3, scene 1, lines 136-139.
[44] Act 3, scene 1, lines 142-146.
[45] Act 3, scene 1, lines 147-149.

What this tells us is that the Self is behind all affect. In the case of Isabella we have witnessed a complete enantiodromia. The mild, merciful, Christian nun becomes a vengeful harpy as she succumbs to possession by what Jungian analysts would call the primitive power animus. At this moment she becomes an unconscious version of Angelo. Like Angelo, Isabella suffers a defeat of her guiding principle, Mercy, because it has encountered something more comprehensive, namely the Self, which we can now recognize as providing the dynamism for the power animus.

As the disguised Duke works behind the scenes the plot takes on more and more complications. Isabella agrees to a rendezvous with Angelo but then arranges for Mariana, his rejected fiancée, to take her place. Angelo, in fear of discovery, violates his agreement and orders Claudio executed and his head presented to him. The disguised Duke prevents the execution and arranges for the head of a prisoner who died of natural causes to be substituted. At this point in the tangled circumstance, the Duke decides to abandon his disguise and reappear.

*3) The Last Judgment: The Self holds the ego accountable*

The final act is a judgment scene. The Duke returns, reveals himself and passes judgment on all concerned, especially Angelo.

In the background of this play looms the ancient traditional image of the Goddess of Justice, in one hand a sword and in the other a balance (as on the Marseille Tarot card shown on the next page). These are both symbols of *separatio,* the process of differentiating and balancing the opposites. The Duke evokes this image in the following passage:

> He who the sword of heaven will bear
> Should be as holy as severe;
> Pattern in himself to know,
> Grace to stand, and virtue, go;
> More nor less to others paying
> Than by self-offenses weighing.

*28 Measure for Measure*

> Shame to him whose cruel striking
> Kills for faults of his own liking!⁴⁶

The Goddess of Justice.
(Marseilles Tarot card)

---

⁴⁶ Act 3, scene 2, lines 254-261.

A psychological paraphrase might run as follows: He who would presume to be the agent of the Self should operate out of a religious attitude generated by self-knowledge and awareness that virtue is a product of grace. He should weigh his own faults in the same balance he uses to judge others based on knowledge of the opposites.

The image of the balance of Justice has its origin in ancient Egyptian religion. The soul of the deceased was subjected to a Last Judgment in which it was weighed on a balance against a feather signifying Maat, the Goddess of Truth. If it balanced, the deceased was escorted victoriously into the presence of Osiris. If not, the soul was fed to a waiting monster. The Egyptian imaging of this (below) was taken over into the medieval Christian symbolism of the Last Judgment (next page) and is deeply ingrained in the Western psyche. Indeed, the whole final Act 5 of *Measure for Measure* is a symbolic version of the Last Judgment.

The soul of the deceased being weighed in the balance.
(From the papyrus of Ani, British Museum; reproduced in
E.A. Wallis Budge, *The Gods of the Egyptians*)

The Archangel Michael weighing souls.
(Van der Weyden, 15th century, Bourgogne, Hospice de Beaume; reproduced in S.G.F. Brandon, *The Judgement of the Dead.*)

## Measure for Measure 31

The climax of the drama comes when the Duke is finally unveiled. Brash, bragging Lucio pulls the hood off the friar's habit that the disguised Duke was wearing. This is the moment of epiphany. Up to now Angelo has been denying Isabella's accusations. Now the jig is up. Like the eye of God that sees all, the disguised Duke has been witness to all his sins. Angelo finally acknowledges his psychic reality.

> Oh, my dread lord,
> I should be guiltier than my guiltiness
> To think I can be undiscernible,
> When I perceive your Grace, like power divine,
> Hath looked upon my passes.[47] Then, good prince,
> No longer session hold upon my shame,
> But let my trial be mine own confession.
> Immediate sentence, then, and sequent death
> Is all the grace I beg.[48]

In this passage Angelo announces his moral salvation. Prior to the Duke's unveiling, Angelo as ego was maintaining his fraudulent innocence, his moral consciousness was in the unconscious. Now comes a crucial point for the understanding of the psyche. Since Angelo was not a psychopath his unconscious was constellated to condemn him.

With the Duke's appearance that missing moral consciousness breaks into awareness, and Angelo, the ego, properly condemns himself. The change in ego-consciousness then changes the attitude of the Self. Now that the ego accepts the justice of its own punishment, the Self becomes merciful. The Duke accepts the pleas for mercy expressed by Mariana and Isabella, and Angelo is forgiven.

---

[47] = trespasses.
[48] Act 5, scene 1, lines 364-372.

## Concluding Remarks

*Measure for Measure* can be seen as a study of the vicissitudes of the ego when it is required to incarnate the Self.

Jung tells us that "the *imago Dei* pervades the whole human sphere and makes mankind its involuntary exponent."[49] Similarly the Duke requires Angelo to embody the image of the Duke, asking, "What figure of us, think you, he will bare?"[50] The Self is the great personality. The ego is the little personality. When the ego is required to incarnate or be the exponent of the great one it is exposed to grave dangers.

> No might nor greatness in mortality
> Can censure 'scape. Back-wounding calumny
> The whitest virtue strikes. What king so strong
> Can tie the gall up in the slanderous tongue?[51]

And again,

> O place and greatness! Millions of false eyes
> Are stuck upon thee: volumes of report
> Run with these false, and most contrarious quest
> Upon thy doings: thousand escapes of wit
> Make thee the father of their idle dream
> And rack thee in their fancies.[52]

These are the outer dangers of greatness deriving from the envy of others. The inner dangers are even greater and can be summed up in one word: inflation. When the ego is inflated, the Self becomes a dangerous adversary because in the long run it will not allow the ego to usurp its authority. Although the ego may be designated as the exponent of the Self, it carries this delegated authority at its peril.

---

[49] "Answer to Job," *Psychology and Religion,* CW 11, par. 660.
[50] Act 1, scene 1, line 16.
[51] Act 3, scene 2, lines 179-182.
[52] Act 4, scene 1, lines 60-65.

The title *Measure for Measure* is an explicit reference to the seventh chapter of Matthew, where Christ says,

> Judge not, that ye be not judged.
> For with what judgment ye judge, ye shall be judged; and with what measure ye mete, it shall be measured to you again.[53]

This idea of a reciprocal relation between the ego and "other" echoes a statement made in Proverbs concerning Divine Wisdom *(Sapientia Dei):*

> Forsake her not, and she shall preserve thee: love her, and she shall keep thee. . . .
> Exalt her, and she shall promote thee: she shall bring thee to honour, when thou dost embrace her.[54]

The same idea appears in alchemy concerning relation to the Philosophers' Stone. A text says,

> Understand ye Sons of Wisdom, the Stone declares: Protect me, and I will protect thee; give me my own, that I may help thee.[55]

Depth psychology has found the same reciprocal relation to apply to the ego's relation to the unconscious. Experience teaches us that the unconscious takes the same attitude toward the ego as the ego shows to it. As Jung says, "In all ordinary cases the unconscious is unfavorable or dangerous only because we are not at one with it and therefore in opposition to it."[56]

The unconscious becomes a dangerous antagonist when the ego usurps the authority of the Self. This is one of the greatest dangers for the ego while it is performing its function as deputy or representative of the Self. The ego is a carrier of authority which is not its own. The misuse of this delegated authority is the basic idea of

---

[53] Matt. 7:1-2.
[54] Prov. 4: 6-8.
[55] "The Golden Treatise of Hermes," in M.A. Atwood, *Hermetic Philosophy and Alchemy,* p. 128.
[56] *Two Essays on Analytical Psychology,* CW 7, par. 195.

the finest passage in the play: Isabella speaks,

> ... man, proud man,
> Dressed in a little brief authority,
> Most ignorant of what he's most assured—
> His glassy essence—like an angry ape
> Played such fantastic tricks before high heaven
> As makes the angels weep;[57]

The punctuation makes clear that "his glassy essence" is what man is most ignorant of.

What is this glassy essence? The commentators are not sure. One suggests it means the rational soul "which reveals to man, as in a mirror, what constitutes him a human being."[58] I have an alchemical association to this term. According to Jung, the alchemists strove to produce an incorruptible "glorified body" which was sometimes *vitrum* (glass).[59] With this amplification we can understand Shakespeare's glassy essence to be a reference to the Self—the inner God-image. It refers alchemically to a glassy pellet that will sometimes be left in the crucible after the contents have undergone a severe process of *calcinatio,* where everything will be burned away and there remains just a little glassy pellet which is impervious to further processing. The eternal essence of the matter must have been treated to produce the glassy essence, image of an incorruptible glorified body. If we go with that association as a reference to the Self, it is of course the end that man is most ignorant of even while he is most assured of it.

Jung describes the Self as a paradoxical union of opposites. The interplay of the opposites is the major feature of *Measure for Measure.* In *Aion,* Jung speaks of the paradoxical Clementine God-image dating back to about 150 A.D.[60] In these writings God is

---

[57] Act 2, scene 2, lines 117-122.
[58] Barnet, ed., *Measure for Measure,* p. 66, footnote.
[59] See *Mysterium Coniunctionis,* CW 14, par. 319.
[60] CW 9ii, par. 99.

*Measure for Measure* 35

pictured as ruling the world with a right and a left hand, the right being Christ, the left Satan. That view is clearly monotheistic, as it unites the opposites in one God.[61]

A similar God-image appears in the Sefirotic Tree of the Kabbala, where the right side is Mercy and the left Judgment. The heretic Marcion in the second century split the paradoxical God-image in half. He maintained that the God of Love, the father of

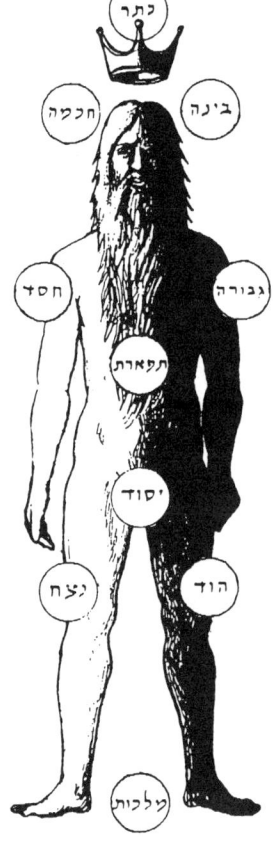

Adam Kadmon and
the Sefirotic Tree.
(From Edward Hoffman,
*The Way of Splendor.*)

---

[61] See "Transformation Symbolism in the Mass," *Psychology and Religion,* CW 11, par. 358, and "Letter to Père Lachat," *The Symbolic Life,* CW 18, par. 1537.

*36 Measure for Measure*

Christ, had nothing to do with Yahweh the God of Law.[62] Orthodox Christianity has steered a wavering course between Clement and Marcion. Jung finally clarified the matter by his empirical discovery of the unconscious paradoxical God-image in the psyche.

These matters are directly relevant to the play. Angelo is an exponent of the harsh God of Judgment, Isabella an exponent of the merciful God of Love. Their conflict reveals what happens when the unconscious, paradoxical Self erupts into consciousness. The Self immediately splits into opposites and presents the ego with the problem of their reconciliation.

It is interesting to note how various characters describe the Duke during his apparent absence. The rascal Lucio describes him thus:

> The Duke had crotchets in him. He would be drunk too.[63]

> [He was] a very superficial, ignorant, unweighing fellow.[64]

> The Duke yet would have dark deeds darkly answered; he would never bring them to light. . . . The Duke, I say to thee again, would eat mutton on Fridays. . . . he would mouth with a beggar though she smelt brown bread and garlic.[65]

On the other hand Escalus, that wise and fair-minded man, speaks of the Duke as one who

> contended especially to know himself . . . . Rather rejoicing to see another merry, than merry at anything which professed to make him rejoice: a gentleman of all temperance.[66]

Understood psychologically, these widely varying appraisals of the Duke correspond to the view of the Self (totality) as seen from different perspectives of the ego. Both descriptions are partially

---

[62] For an extensive commentary on Marcion's ideas, see Edinger, *The Psyche in Antiquity, Book Two: Gnosticism and Early Christianity,* chap. 4.
[63] Act 3, scene 2, line 124. "Crochets" are whims, odd notions.
[64] Act 3, scene 2, line 136.
[65] Act 3, scene 2, lines 170ff. "Mutton" is slang for whore; to eat mutton on Fridays means to eat forbidden meat, that is, have recourse to prostitutes.
[66] Act 3, scene 2, lines 226ff.

true. When they are combined they give us a picture of what Jung calls the paradoxical God-image, which is beyond the grasp and understanding of the ego. In the course of the play the opposites are reconciled. By the end all the major figures, including the Duke, have undergone transformation and have lost their original one-sidedness. This occurs through the agency of the *coniunctio* archetype. The play ends with a fourfold *coniunctio*.

In the final chapter of *Mysterium Coniunctionis* Jung discusses the *coniunctio* as a three-stage process. The first stage is called the *unio mentalis* and is associated with the symbolism of beheading. Interestingly this image of decapitation has a prominent place in the play. Angelo orders Claudio beheaded and he is spared that fate only through the substitution of another prisoner who has died of natural causes. It is the head of this substitute that is then presented to Angelo, like the head of John the Baptist to Salome.

The theme of decapitation is highly relevant to the subject matter of this story, which is the conflict between body and spirit. Angelo and Isabella in their different ways had both separated the head from the body. At the other end of the spectrum, the whorehouse psychology of Mistress Overdone and her pimp Pompey had likewise separated the body from the head. According to Jung decapitation symbolism belongs to what he calls the first stage of the *coniunctio,* the so-called *unio mentalis.* He writes,

> In order to bring about their subsequent reunion, the mind *(mens)* must be separated from the body—which is equivalent to "voluntary death"—for only separated things can unite. . . . The aim of this separation was to free the mind from the influence of the "bodily appetites and the heart's affections," and to establish a spiritual position which is supraordinate to the turbulent sphere of the body. This leads at first to a dissociation of the personality and a violation of the merely natural man.[67]

The symbolic image for this process is beheading. Again Jung:

---

[67] *Mysterium Coniunctionis,* CW 14, par. 671.

Beheading is significant symbolically as the separation of the "understanding" from the "great suffering and grief" which nature inflicts on the soul. It is an emancipation of the "cogitatio" which is situated in the head, a freeing of the soul from the "trammels of nature." Its purpose is to bring about . . . a *unio mentalis* "in the overcoming of the body."[68]

The second stage of the *coniunctio* is a reconnection of the separated opposites represented by the *unio mentalis* (the united soul and spirit) on the one hand and the body on the other. In *Measure for Measure* this is expressed by the fourfold *coniunctio* with which the play ends:

> Claudio is united with Juliet
> Angelo is united with Mariana
> Lucio is united with a prostitute
> The Duke is united with Isabella

It is also interesting to note that the basic plot is triggered by an "illegitimate" *coniunctio,* one gone wrong, so to speak, in the love affair of Claudio and Juliet. Only once before has Shakespeare used the name Juliet—in his other *coniunctio* drama, *Romeo and Juliet.* Surely this is significant.

For those interested in the personal aspect of psychological imagery, an event in Shakespeare's adolescence, as described by A.L. Rowse, will also be relevant:

> Towards the end of August 1582, at the mature age of eighteen, he got Anne Hathaway with child, a spinster eight years older . . . . She was of a respectable parentage and had to be married . . . . By November . . . it was clear that she was pregnant . . . [so] William and Anne were married on 30 November or 1 December.[69]

The phenomenology of the *coniunctio* archetype is present

---

[68] Ibid., par. 730. For more on the motif of beheading, see Edinger, *The Mysterium Lectures: A Journey through C.G. Jung's* Mysterium Coniunctionis, pp. 302ff.
[69] *William Shakespeare: A Biography,* pp. 56f.

throughout the play. The prominence of the opposites and frequent enantiodromias are characteristic, as are the many references to Eros, from the bawdy to the sublime.

In the very final passage there is a grand reconciliation characteristic of the climax of the *coniunctio,* concluding with these words spoken by the Duke:

> Dear Isabel,
> I have a motion much imports your good;
> Wereto if you'll a willing ear incline,
> What's mine is yours and what is yours is mine.
> So bring us to our palace; where we'll show
> What's yet behind, that's meet you all should know.[70]

Like Yahweh who chooses Israel to be his bride, so the Duke as the Self chooses Isabella, as feminine ego to be his conscious living partner and promises to reveal to her yet undisclosed secrets. This echoes a passage in Ecclesiasticus which speaks of the fruits of a relation to Divine Wisdom:

> Whoever obeys her judges aright,
>     and whoever pays attention to her dwells secure.
> If he trusts himself to her he will inherit her,
>     and his descendants will remain in possession of her;
> for though she takes him at first through winding ways,
>     Bringing fear and faintness on him,
> plaguing him with her discipline until she can trust him,
>     and testing him with her ordeals,
> in the end she will lead him back to the straight road,
>     and reveal her secrets to him.[71]

Finally, I think it is instructive to consider what the figure of the Duke teaches us about the nature of the Self as revealed through Shakespeare's imagination. He has been a problem for Shakespeare scholars. As one puts it,

---

[70] Act 5, scene 1, lines 531-536.
[71] Ecclus. 4:15ff.

> The role of the Duke is not clearly defined. Although he conforms to the literary tradition of the Disguised Ruler, no satisfactory reason is given for his temporary abdication. . . . The Duke could assert his identify at any time and free Claudio from prison, but he elects to play devious games and allows the young man to arrive at the very brink of death before stepping in. He also engages in a cat-and-mouse game with Isabella, concealing the fact that Claudio is alive and thus causing her needless anguish.[72]

These are the common reactions of rational consciousness when confronted with the trickster aspect of the unconscious. Despite these ambiguities, some scholars have equated the Duke with Christ. The very title is a paraphrase of the words of Jesus:

> Judge not that ye be not judged.
> For with what judgement ye judge, ye shall be judged: and with what measure ye mete, it shall be measured to you again.[73]

In spite of these parallels the figure of the Duke is not adequately explained as a Christ figure, at least not in the traditional, orthodox sense. In fact the behavior of the Duke does not at all fit the conventional God-image. However it *does* fit the empirical God-image as described by Jung. This God-image is paradoxical and needs individual ego-consciousness for its realization. Jung says, "God can be called good only inasmuch as He is able to manifest His goodness in individuals."[74] The same idea seems to apply to the Duke concerning justice. The Duke is able to achieve justice, the balance of the opposites, only by delegating this task to his deputy, Angelo, the ego. This task is too much for the ego, as it always is, but in the failure of the ego, the conscious realization of the Self is born. The Duke returns and there is an apocatastasis, a restoration of all things, as proclaimed in the New Testament.[75]

---

[72] David M. Zesmer, *Guide to Shakespeare,* p. 293.
[73] Matt. 7:1-2.
[74] *C.G. Jung Letters,* vol. 2, p. 314.
[75] Acts 3:20-21.

Jung translates this into psychological terms. Referring to a damaged God-image in man that can be reformed, or transformed, with the help of God, in accordance with Romans 12:2,[76] he writes:

> The totality images which the unconscious produces in the course of an individuation process are similar "reformations" of an *a priori* archetype.... The spontaneous symbols of the self, or of wholeness, cannot in practice be distinguished from a God-image.... The "renewal" ... of the mind is not meant as an actual alteration of consciousness, but rather as the restoration of an original condition, an apocatastasis. This is in exact agreement with the empirical findings of psychology, that there is an ever-present archetype of wholeness which may easily disappear from the purview of consciousness or may never be perceived at all until a consciousness illuminated by conversion recognizes it in the figure of Christ [or some other Self-figure]. As a result of this "anamnesis" the original state of oneness with the God-image is restored. It brings about an integration, a bridging of the split in the personality caused by the instincts striving apart in different and mutually contradictory directions.[77]

---

[76] "And be not conformed to this world, but be transformed by the renewal of your mind, that you may prove what is ... the will of God." (Revised Standard Version)
[77] *Aion,* CW 9ii., par. 73.

# *Romeo and Juliet*
# A Coniunctio Drama

A warring peace, a sweet wound, a mild evil.
—C.G. Jung, "The Psychology of the Transference."

# Foreword

At first it seemed illogical to me that this should be the second essay in this book, rather than the end piece, because the *coniunctio* is generally the culmination of the alchemical opus.

However, although the major *coniunctio* themes in *Romeo and Juliet*—love, war, beauty, marriage, death and the union of opposites—are the same as those addressed in the final essay on Oedipus, here they are shown to have a lesser magnitude. This is in line with Edinger's concepts of a "lesser" and a "greater" *coniunctio*, which he distinguishes and clarifies in the language of alchemy:

> In attempting to understand the rich and complex symbolism of the *coniunctio* it is advisable to distinguish two phases: a lesser *coniunctio* and a greater. The lesser *coniunctio* is a union or fusion of substances that are not yet thoroughly separated or discriminated. It is always followed by death or *mortificatio*. The greater *coniunctio*, on the other hand, is the goal of the *opus*, the supreme accomplishment. In actual reality these two aspects are combined with each other. The experience of the *coniunctio* is almost always a mixture of the lesser and the greater aspects.[78]

Thus, ordering the essays in this way corresponds to the process of individuation, the ordering principle of the psyche. This gives us an opportunity to examine both levels of the mystery of the *coniunctio*, and to understand similarities and differences.

In *Romeo and Juliet*, two young lovers become caught up in the explosive archetypal energy of their warring families. Despite their heroic efforts to reconcile the opposites, they are cruelly ground between them. Both are defeated by death—sacrificed to the enmity of their families.

Symbolically, their death might have been the prelude to rebirth,

---

[78] *Anatomy of the Psyche: Alchemical Symbolism in Psychotherapy*, p. 211.

as it is in Romeo's dream (below, page 63), in which he sees an image of the Self born out of the death of the ego ("And all this day an unaccustom'd spirit / Lifts me above the ground with cheerful thoughts / . . . [And so] I reviv'd, and was an emperor"). The image pictures coming events on a spiritual plane. Historically, we experience a certain truth to the image of afterlife in Romeo's dream because his story is eternal, mythic and "reviv'd" in our own time.

Edinger concludes that although in terms of the ego Romeo and Juliet are defeated by death, beyond the personal ego realm they are victorious. Theirs is a circumambulation of the *unus mundus,* absent the great transformation that would have made it possible for them to embody and *live* in relation to the archetype that their lives bodied forth for the rest of us. This is the "lesser" *coniunctio.*

The original manuscript for this essay was written as a gift for a Festschrift in honor of Edinger's colleague Joseph Henderson, who comments on it as follows:

> [When Romeo and Juliet die] their love survives as the eternal promise of some ultimate union to be achieved on a higher plane than could be satisfied in this life by love alone. Edward Edinger has shown, in a brilliant interpretation of *Romeo and Juliet,* that the power of that relationship lies in embodying an alchemical *coniunctio* or union of opposites that does in fact lift this otherwise simple tale of adolescent love to such a height of symbolic meaning. From this point of view any love story only becomes truly meaningful from its archetypal content, not just from its outer manifestation, and the more its outer realization is frustrated, the more significant may be its inner image.[79]

Here, then, is Edinger's masterful analysis of *The Tragedy of Romeo and Juliet.*

*Sheila Dickman Zarrow*

---

[79] *Cultural Attitudes in Psychological Perspective,* pp. 102f.

## Introduction

Shakespeare's *Romeo and Juliet* is a work open to many interpretations. On the deepest level it can be seen as a drama of the mystery of the *coniunctio*. Its major themes—love, war, beauty, marriage, death and the union of opposites—are all related to this archetype. The interplay and paradoxical union of opposites is a particularly prominent motif, appearing in Romeo's first speech:

> Here's much to do with hate, but more with love:
> Why, then, O brawling love! O loving hate!
> O anything! of nothing first create!
> O heavy lightness! serious vanity!
> Mis-shapen chaos of well-seeming forms!
> Feather of lead, bright smoke, cold fire, sick health!
> Still-waking sleep, that is not what it is![80]

This passage is reminiscent of the quotation that Jung chose as a motto for his study of *coniunctio* symbolism in "The Psychology of the Transference":

> *Bellica pax, vulnus dulce, suave malum*
> (A warring peace, a sweet wound, a mild evil)[81]

The parallel does not end there. As we shall see, in still other respects *Romeo and Juliet* corresponds symbolically with the series of pictures from the *Rosarium philosophorum* which Jung discusses in that essay.

The play begins with a prologue by the Chorus which outlines the plot with brevity and beauty:

> Two households, both alike in dignity,
>   In fair Verona, where we lay our scene,

---

[80] Act 1, scene 1, lines 174-180.
[81] *The Practice of Psychotherapy,* CW 16, preceding par. 353.

> From ancient grudge break to new mutiny,
>   Where civil blood makes civil hands unclean.
> From forth the fatal loins of these two foes
>   A pair of star-cross'd lovers take their life;
> Whose misadventur'd piteous overthrows
>   Do with their death bury their parents' strife.
> The fearful passage of their death-mark'd love,
>   And the continuance of their parents' rage,
> Which, but their children's end nought could remove,
>   Is now the two hours' traffick of our stage.

The play concerns, we are told, a new outbreak of an "ancient grudge." It is as though the conflict between the houses of Montague and Capulet represents a current, personal version of the archetypal strife between the opposites. The created world began with a separation of opposites. ("God divided the light from the darkness."—Gen. 1:4.) That initial *separatio,* the tearing apart of the united opposites, was a crime, and hence the Milesian philosopher Anaximander can speak of the "injustice" incurred by the existence of separate things.[82] The existence of the ego is based on the separation and perpetual conflict of the opposites. This is the original sin, the ancient grudge that breaks out again and again in new and unexpected forms.

Every major increase of consciousness involves a reawakening of that ancient grudge. It corresponds to the psychological condition that Jung speaks of, which

> occurs when the analysis has constellated the opposites so powerfully that a union or synthesis of the personality becomes an imperative necessity.... [A conflict is generated that] requires a real

---

[82] "The Non-Limited *(Apeiron)* is the original material of existing things, further, the source from which existing things derive their existence is also that to which they return at their destruction, according to necessity; for they give justice and make reparation to one another for their injustice, according to the arrangement of Time." (Kathleen Freeman, *Ancilla to the Pre-Socratic Philsophers,* p. 19) For more information on Anaximander, see Edinger, *The Psyche in Antiquity, Book One: Early Greek Philosophy,* pp. 20ff.

solution and necessitates a third thing in which the opposites can unite.... In nature the resolution of opposites is always an energic process.[83]

## A Psychological Study of the Play

Romeo and Juliet are personifications of the constellated opposites, and the third thing which arises between them, the energic process that resolves the conflict, is love. This corresponds to the dove descending between the king and queen in the first of the *Rosarium* pictures (next page).[84]

*Romeo and Juliet* concerns the *mysterium amoris*. Since this is a manifestation of the *numinosum* it defies rational description. As Jung says:

> I falter before the task of finding the language which might adequately express the incalculable paradoxes of love. Eros is a *kosmogonos,* a creator and father-mother of all higher consciousness.... I have again and again been faced with the mystery of love, and have never been able to explain what it is. Like Job, I had to "lay my hand on my mouth. I have spoken once, and I will not answer." (Job 40: 4f.) ... For we are in the deepest sense the victims and the instruments of cosmogonic "love."[85]

The encounter with Eros, the mighty daimon, occurs early in the play. For Romeo, love was generated by beauty, which might be defined as the aesthetic aspect of the *numinosum*. Rilke's lines in the first of his *Duino Elegies* are relevant here:

> For Beauty's nothing
> but beginning of Terror we're still just able to bear,
> and why we adore it so is because it serenely
> disdains to destroy us. Every angel is terrible.[86]

---

[83] *Mysterium Coniunctionis,* CW 14, par. 705.
[84] The *Rosarium* pictures reproduced in this essay are taken from "The Psychology of the Transference," *The Practice of Psychotherapy,* CW 16.
[85] *Memories, Dreams, Reflections,* pp. 353f.
[86] J.B. Leishman, ed. and trans., *Rilke: Selected Poems,* p. 60.

# PHILOSOPHORVM.

Nota bene: In arte noſtri magiſterij nihil eſt **Secretum**
celatū à Philoſophis excepto ſecreto artis, quod **artis**
non licet cuiquam reuelare, quod ſi fieret ille ma
lediceretur, & indignationem domini incur﹔
reret, & apoplexia moreretur. ⁜ Quare om﹔
nis error in arte exiſtit, ex eo, quod debitam

Dove descending between king and queen.
(From *Rosarium philosophorum*, in CW 16, p. 213.)

The passage describing Romeo's first reaction to Juliet's beauty is itself exquisitely beautiful, a magnificent wedding of form and content. Beauty is described by beauty.

> What lady is that which doth enrich the hand
> of yonder knight? . . .
> O! she doth teach the torches to burn bright.
> It seems she hangs upon the cheek of night
> Like a rich jewel in an Ethiop's ear:
> Beauty too rich for use, for earth too dear![87]

Love and beauty are transpersonal factors, evoking a sense of the divine. Thus, at their first meeting, Romeo and Juliet speak to each other in religious terms. He says,

> If I profane with my unworthiest hand
> This holy shrine, the gentle sin is this;
> My lips, two blushing pilgrims, ready stand
> To smooth that rough touch with a tender kiss.[88]

And Juliet replies,

> Good pilgrim, you do wrong your hand too much
> Which mannerly devotion shows in this;
> For saints have hands that pilgrims' hands do touch,
> And palm to palm is holy palmers' kiss.[89]

But transpersonal factors are dangerous; a holy shrine is charged with *mana*.[90] Like the tabernacle of Yahweh, it has destructive effects if approached carelessly. A meeting between the lesser (the ego) and the greater (the Self) is indeed the "fearful passage" described in the opening lines of the play. The risk is that the lesser will be dissolved by the greater. This accounts for the symbolic

---

[87] Act 1, scene 5, lines 42-47.
[88] Act 1, scene 5, lines 93-96.
[89] Act 1, scene 5, lines 97-100.
[90] *[Mana* is a Melanesian word referring to a bewitching or numinous quality in gods or sacred objects.—Ed.]

*52 Romeo and Juliet*

connection between love and death. *Romeo and Juliet* is a rich study in this linkage.[91]

Love threatens one with loss of identity. If love is based on the projection of an archetypal image, perhaps the Self, then to unite with the loved one threatens dissolution of the ego-self. In one dialogue Romeo's identity, that is, his name, is specifically at issue. Juliet speaks the lines now so familiar to us:

> O Romeo, Romeo! wherefore art thou Romeo?
> Deny thy father and refuse thy name:
> . . . .
> 'Tis but thy name that is my enemy;
> Thou art thyself though, not a Montague.
> What's Montague? it is nor hand, nor foot,
> Nor arm, nor face, nor any other part
> Belonging to a man. O! be some other name:
> What's in a name? that which we call a rose
> By any other name would smell as sweet;
> . . . . Romeo, doff thy name;
> And for thy name, which is no part of thee,
> Take all myself.[92]

Romeo responds:

> I take thee at thy word.
> Call me but love, and I'll be new baptiz'd;
> Henceforth I never will be Romeo.[93]

This willingness to relinquish his identity is dubious, at least from the standpoint of the ego. Romeo asks to be called love; that is, he identifies with the archetype. As Jung tells us, this can lead to dismemberment:

---

[91] [Naturally, anima/animus projections play a large part in the attraction between Romeo and Juliet, as they do in any "love at first sight" situation. But clearly, in this essay, the author is concerned with deeper issues.—Ed.]
[92] Act 2, scene 2, lines 33-48.
[93] Act 2, scene 2, lines 49-51.

When the *spiritus phantasticus* in man, his creative phantasy, reaches beyond man in any respect, below or above, he really becomes divine. Then Synesius says an extraordinary thing: he says, "And being divine, he has, as such, to undergo the divine punishment." And the divine punishment is dismemberment: he will be torn in pieces, he will be sacrificed like a sacrificial animal that is cut asunder upon the altar.[94]

Romeo and Juliet are both sacrificial victims. They fall into identification with the archetype of *coniunctio* and are thus fated for dismemberment. At the conclusion of the play Capulet calls them "poor sacrifices of our enmity!"[95]

At one point, Romeo's rage against his name takes on the proportions of madness. After he has killed Tybalt and hears that Juliet is weeping and calling out his name, he vents his despair:

> As if that name,
> Shot from the deadly level of a gun,
> Did murder her; as that name's cursed hand
> Murder'd her kinsman. O! tell me, friar, tell me,
> In what vile part of this anatomy
> Doth my name lodge? tell me that I may sack
> The hateful mansion. [Drawing his sword][96]

Romeo has been inundated by more self-knowledge than he can stand. He would annihilate his identity, the "hateful mansion" of his name. As Jung has said,

> The way to yourself is the longest way and the hardest way. Everybody would pay anything, his whole fortune, to avoid going to himself. Most people hate themselves, despise themselves, and for nothing in the world would they go where they are, where their native town is, because it is just hell![97]

---

[94] *The Visions Seminars,* vol. 1, p. 85. [Synesius of Edessa was an early Christian philosopher who lived between the fifth and sixth centuries.—Ed.]
[95] Act 5, scene 3, line 304.
[96] Act 3, scene 3, lines 102-108.
[97] *The Visions Seminars,* vol. 1, p. 30.

## 54  Romeo and Juliet

Romeo's loss of his name also has a positive side. He is no longer confined to a narrow, one-sided identity. His love for Juliet has released him from the Montague-Capulet conflict. He is no longer identified with one side of a pair of warring opposites. However, his friend Mercutio (his shadow) is not so released. Mercutio is an aggressive, high-spirited figure who plays at shadow projection and stirs up dissension wherever he goes.

In act 2, scene 4, Mercutio, in his usual manner, fences with Romeo intellectually, engaging in the thrust and parry of witticisms. At one point he exclaims, "Come between us, good Benvolio; my wit faints."[98] This theme of "coming between" the warring opposites occurs again in graven form in act 3, scene 1, where Tybalt tries to provoke Romeo to fight. But Romeo will not be baited by Tybalt's insults. His love for Juliet lets him see Tybalt as a brother. For the moment, he is beyond the conflict of the opposites.

Mercutio, however, is incensed at Romeo's composure. As is characteristic of the one-sided partisan, Mercutio interprets Romeo's position beyond the opposites as weakness and exclaims scornfully, "O calm, dishonourable, vile submission!"[99] Mercutio then provokes Tybalt and they fight. Romeo comes between them in an effort to stop the fight. Instead, Mercutio is mortally wounded under Romeo's arm

It is a fearful thing to come between the warring opposites. Romeo had had a glimpse of a wholeness beyond the opposites, but had overestimated the strength of his position. His insight was not yet effectively realized.

When Mercutio is dying, he and Romeo exchange standpoints. Mercutio achieves an attitude beyond the opposites, expressed negatively in the words, "a plague on both your houses."[100] Romeo,

---

[98] Act 2, scene 4, line 69.
[99] Act 3, scene 1, line 72.
[100] Act 3, scene 1, line 98.

however, regresses to Mercutio's earlier state of identification with the conflict.

Such a regression is a typical transient phenomenon during the integration of the shadow. Having been indirectly responsible for the death of Mercutio by stepping between the opposites, Romeo must now assume the responsibility for correcting the balance. Coming between the opposites makes one the carrier of wholeness, a divine burden, which, if shouldered unconsciously, has tragic consequences. Thus could Romeo well declare after killing Tybalt, "O! I am Fortune's fool."[101]

Romeo is caught in the coils of a tragic process. Significantly, the theme of dismemberment now makes its first appearance. Just before the nurse announces Tybalt's death to Juliet, the latter, in the midst of an apostrophe to night, exclaims:

> Give me my Romeo: and, when he shall die,
> Take him and cut him out in little stars,
> And he will make the face of heaven so fine
> That all the world will be in love with night,
> And pay no worship to the garish sun.[102]

When Romeo pours out his suicidal despair to Friar Lawrence, the friar replies:

> Fie, fie! thou sham'st thy shape, thy love, thy wit
> . . . .
> Thy wit, that ornament to shape and love,
> Misshapen in the conduct of them both,
> Like powder in a skilless soldier's flask,
> Is set a-fire by thine own ignorance,
> And thou dismember'd with thine own defence.[103]

And finally Romeo, in the last stage of his desperation, about to

---

[101] Act 3, scene 1, line 135.
[102] Act 3, scene 2, lines 21-25.
[103] Act 3, scene 3, lines 122-134.

## 56 Romeo and Juliet

enter Juliet's tomb, warns Balthasar not to spy on him.

> But if thou, jealous, dost return to pry
> In what I further shall intend to do,
> By heaven, I will tear thee joint by joint,
> And strew this hungry churchyard with thy limbs.
> The time and my intents are savage-wild,
> More fierce and more inexorable far
> Than empty tigers or the roaring sea.[104]

Romeo is the dismembered one. He has been rent asunder by his desires and their frustration, the yea and nay of the archetypal opposites. This is the consequence of identifying with archetypal love, coming between the opposites and carelessly entering the divine region of wholeness. Like the huntsman Actaeon, torn apart and devoured by dogs because he chanced to see Artemis in her naked glory, Romeo encountered the transpersonal unexpectedly and was dismembered by his own hounds (instinctual passions).

Dismemberment is one of the consequences of the alchemical *coniunctio*. Jung writes (quoting from the Vision of Arisleus):[105]

> "With so much love did Beya embrace Gabricus that she absorbed him wholly into her own nature and dissolved him into indivisible particles." Ripley says that at the death of the king all his limbs were torn into "atoms." This is the motif of dismemberment which is well known in alchemy. The atoms are or become "white sparks" shining in the *terra foetida* [stench of the graves]. They are also called the "fishes' eyes."[106]

Analogous to dismemberment is the theme of igniting gunpowder, which is used several times. In addition to the friar's reference to "powder in a skilless soldier's flask," he had earlier cautioned Romeo to mitigate his urgent desires, in these words:

---

[104] Act 5, scene 3, lines 33-39.
[105] See *Psychology and Alchemy,* CW 12, pars. 435ff, 449f; also Edinger, *The Mysterium Lectures,* pp. 84ff.
[106] *Mysterium Coniunctionis,* CW 14, par. 64.

The slaying of the king.
(From Stolcius de Stolcenberg, *Viridarium chymicum*, 1642.)

> These violent delights have violent ends
> And in their triumph die, like fire and powder,
> Which, as they kiss, consume.[107]

Again, when Romeo is buying poison from the apothecary, he says,

> Let me have
> A dram of poison, such soon-speeding gear
> As will disperse itself through all the veins
> That the life-weary taker may fall dead,
> And that the trunk may be discharg'd of breath
> As violently as hasty powder fir'd
> Doth hurry from the fatal cannon's womb.[108]

Gunpowder represents the explosive energy charge contained in an archetype. No sooner does an immature ego touch the archetype than it becomes inflated and in danger of being exploded by its transpersonal energy. Both Romeo and Juliet have fallen into the archetypal realm of the *coniunctio* and, in their immaturity, are cruelly ground between the opposites.

When Juliet first learns that Romeo has killed her cousin Tybalt, she is burdened with a load of opposites beyond her ability to bear. She expresses her agony in these lines:

> O serpent heart, hid with a flowering face!
> Did ever dragon keep so fair a cave?
> Beautiful tyrant! fiend angelical!
> Dove-feather'd raven! wolvish-ravening lamb!
> Despised substance of divinest show!
> Just opposite to what thou justly seem'st;
> A damned saint, an honourable villain!
> O, nature! what hadst thou to do in hell
> When thou didst bower the spirit of a fiend
> In mortal paradise of such sweet flesh?
> Was ever book containing such vile matter

---

[107] Act 2, scene 6, lines 9-11.
[108] Act 5, scene 1, lines 59-65.

> So fairly bound? O! that deceit should dwell
> In such a gorgeous palace.[109]

Juliet awakens quickly from this frantic state and recovers her personal feelings for Romeo. However, she had momentarily projected onto Romeo the paradoxical and awesome qualities of the *coniunctio*. Similarly, Romeo falls into a frenzy upon learning of his banishment. Fate has tossed him violently back and forth between the opposites. Heaven is where Juliet is; hell is her absence.

> There is no world without Verona walls,
> But purgatory, torture, hell itself.
> Hence banished is banish'd from the world,
> And world's exile is death; then "banished"
> Is death mis-termed. Calling death "banished,"
> Thou cut'st my head off with a golden axe,
> And smil'st upon the stroke that murders me.[110]
>
> "Banished!"
> O friar! the damned use that word in hell;
> Howling attends it.[111]

For the once-born ego, encounter with the *coniunctio* appears first as heaven and then as death. *Romeo and Juliet* is one of our most explicit literary expressions of that fact. The equation "marriage equals death" runs like a black thread through the play. When Romeo first urges Friar Lawrence to marry them, he says,

> Do thou but close our hands with holy words,
> Then love-devouring death do what he dare;
> It is enough I may but call her mine.[112]

When Juliet is found apparently dead, her father Capulet exclaims to Paris,

---

[109] Act 3, scene 2, lines 73-85.
[110] Act 3, scene 2, lines 17-23.
[111] Act 3, scene 3, lines 47-49.
[112] Act 2, scene 6, lines 6-8.

> O Son! the night before thy wedding-day
> Hath Death lain with thy wife. There she lies,
> Flower as she was, deflowered by him.
> Death is my son-in-law, Death is my heir;
> My daughter he hath wedded: I will die,
> And leave him all; life, living, all is Death's![113]

The wedding has turned into a funeral.

> All things that we ordained festival,
> Turn from their office to black funeral;
> Our instruments to melancholy bells,
> Our wedding cheer to a sad burial feast,
> Our solemn hymns to sullen dirges change,
> Our bridal flowers serve for a buried corse,
> And all things change them to the contrary.[114]

Finally, in the last scene of the play, Romeo wonders at Juliet's beauty in the tomb.

> Ah! dear Juliet,
> Why art though yet so fair? Shall I believe
> That unsubstantial Death is amorous,
> And that the lean abhorred monster keeps
> Thee here in dark to be his paramour?[115]

The theme of marriage to death is widespread in myth and folklore, for instance Persephone's abduction by Hades and the tale of Amor and Psyche. Alchemical imagery also frequently connects marriage or sexual union with death. An example is the series of pictures from the *Rosarium philosophorum*. In this series, the picture following sexual union shows the king and queen, merged into one figure, lying dead in the tomb (opposite). Concerning this symbolism, Jung writes:

---

[113] Act 4, scene 5, lines 35-40.
[114] Act 4, scene 5, lines 84-90.
[115] Act 5, scene 3, lines 101-105.

# PHILOSOPHORVM.
## CONCEPTIO SEV PVTRE*factio*

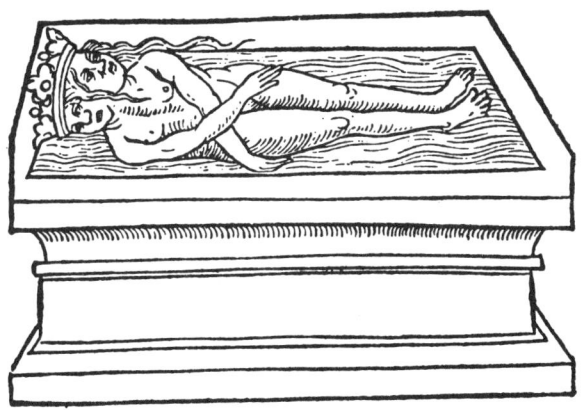

Hye ligen könig vnd köningin dot/
Die sele scheydt sich mit grosser not.

## ARISTOTELES REX ET *Philosophus.*

Nunquam vidi aliquod animatum crescere sine putrefactione, nisi autem fiat putri׃ dum inuanum erit opus alchimicum.

*Here King and Queen are lying dead /*
*In great distress the soul is sped.*

King and queen lying dead in the tomb.
(From *Rosarium philosophorum*, in CW 16, p. 259.)

> The integration of contents that were always unconscious and projected involves a serious lesion of the ego. Alchemy expresses this through the symbols of death, mutilation, or poisoning.[116]

We have seen how both Romeo and Juliet were "poisoned" by their encounter with the united opposites. But yet the ultimate meaning is not negative. During a process that unites the opposites, that is, individuation, good and evil can often be paradoxically reversed. Friar Lawrence sounds this theme explicitly in his panegyric to the herbs and minerals of the earth:

> For nought so vile that on the earth doth live
> But to the earth some special good doth give,
> Nor aught so good but, strain'd from that fair use,
> Revolts from true birth, stumbling on abuse
> Virtue itself turns vice, being misapplied,
> And vice sometime's by action dignified.
> Within the infant rind of this weak flower
> Poison hath residence and medicine power;
> . . . .
> Two such opposed kings encamp them still
> In man as well as herbs, grace and rude will.[117]

"Grace" and "rude will" correspond to the two basic modes of psychic being, love and power. As Jung says,

> Where love reigns, there is no will to power; and where the will to power is paramount, love is lacking. The one is but the shadow of the other.[118]

Each of these modes can be lived at different levels, from the most primitive to the most differentiated. They are a pair of opposites, equal in value and importance. Power promotes differentiation, separateness, knowledge, and the individualized ego. Love

---

[116] "The Psychology of the Transference," *The Practice of Psychotherapy,* CW 16, par. 472.
[117] Act 2, scene 3, lines 16-28.
[118] *Two Essays on Analytical Psychology,* CW 7, par. 78.

promotes union, intimacy, social interest, and relation to the transpersonal. As a pair of opposites they are contradictory. The truth of one is the falsehood of the other. To win in the power mode is to lose in love. Thus Juliet says, while waiting for her lover,

> Come, civil night,
> Thou sober-suited matron, all in black,
> And learn me how to lose a winning match,
> Play'd for a pair of stainless maidenhoods.[119]

Romeo and Juliet both lose a winning match. In ego-power terms they are defeated by death. However, in transpersonal-love terms they are victorious.

Symbolically, death is the prelude to rebirth. Notes Jung, "The alchemists assert that death is at once the conception of the *filius philosophorum,*"[120] which is to say, the realization of the Self is born out of the death of the ego. Thus in the *Rosarium* pictures death is followed by resurrection (next page). Rebirth following death is also suggested in *Romeo and Juliet*. The reconciliation of Capulet and Montague is an expression of life reborn from the deaths of their children, "poor sacrifices of [their] enmity!"[121]

Also, there is Romeo's rebirth dream, which pictures the coming events from the standpoint of the unconscious.

> My dreams presage some joyful news at hand:
> My bosom's lord sits lightly in his throne;
> And all this day an unaccustom'd spirit
> Lifts me above the ground with cheerful thoughts.
> I dreamt my lady came and found me dead;—
> Strange dream, that gives a dead man leave to think,—
> And breath'd such life with kisses in my lips,
> That I reviv'd, and was an emperor.[122]

---

[119] Act 3, scene 2, lines 10-13.
[120] "The Psychology of the Transference," *The Practice of Psychotherapy,* CW 16, par. 473.
[121] Act 5, scene 3, line 304.
[122] Act 5, scene 1, lines 2-9.

# PHILOSOPHORVM.

Hie ist geboren die eddele Keyserin reich/
Die meister nennen sie jhrer dochter gleich.
Die vermeret sich/gebiert kinder ohn zal/
Sein vnd ötlich rein/vnnd ohn alles mahl.

*Here is born the Empress of all honour /*
*The philosophers name her their daughter.*
*She multiplies / bears children ever again /*
*They are incorruptibly pure and without stain.*

The new birth.
(From *Rosarium philosophorum,* in CW 16, p. 307.)

## Concluding Remarks

In the end, *Romeo and Juliet* leaves one with the definite sense of life and love triumphant over death. Donald Stauffer, the Shakespearean scholar, notes this fact:

> The intensity of their single-souled impulse has turned their passion into a death-devouring love. . . . Man's deeper instincts play strange juggleries in attaining truth beyond the reach of metaphysics, so that there is a mysterious authenticity in Romeo's phrase "a triumphant grave". . . . The sense of triumph descends upon the play from a love so straight, so simple, and so certain that its very bravery transforms death and time and hatred—yes, and the accidents of fate—into insubstantial shadows. The quick bright things remain shining and alive.[123]

The "triumphant grave" passage occurs as Romeo lays dead Paris in Juliet's tomb:

> O! give me thy hand,
> One writ with me in sour misfortune's book:
> I'll bury thee in a triumphant grave;
> A grave? O, no! a lanthorn, slaughter'd youth,
> For here lies Juliet, and her beauty makes
> This vault a feasting presence full of light.[124]

It has been noted that *Romeo and Juliet* is unusual among Shakespeare's plays for the number of references it makes to light.[125] And almost all of these link light to beauty as occurs here where Juliet's beauty is described as "a feasting presence full of light."

Keats has taught us that beauty is truth. For Shakespeare, beauty is light. If light refers symbolically to consciousness, then consciousness is beautiful. And also, we can say, beauty promotes consciousness. The fine arts can thus be seen as great collective carriers

---

[123] *Shakespeare's World of Images,* p. 59.
[124] Act 5, scene 3, lines 81-86.
[125] See Caroline F.E. Spurgeon, *Shakespeare's Imagery and What It Tells Us,* p. 312.

of consciousness. Strictly speaking, of course, only individuals carry consciousness. Works of art *transmit* consciousness from the artist to the perceiver if the latter is ready to receive it. Certainly this play, in its beauty, is a bringer of consciousness.

If there was an historical Romeo and Juliet, they did not die in vain. Their lives have bodied forth an archetype for the benefit of all. The following lines spoken by Juliet (quoted earlier, modified here to apply to both), picture their translation to eternity and their everlasting witness to the light that shines in the darkness.

> And, when they shall die,
> Take them and cut them out in little stars,
> And they will make the face of heaven so fine
> That all the world will be in love with night,
> And pay no worship to the garish sun.[126]

---

## Publisher's Note

For more extensive commentaries by Edward F. Edinger on the *coniunctio* theme, readers are referred to these two Inner City titles:

*The Mystery of the Coniunctio: Alchemical Image of Individuation.* (1994) 112 pages. **48 illustrations.**

*The Mysterium Lectures: A Journey through C.G. Jung's* Mysterium Coniunctionis. (1995) 352 pages. **90 illustrations.**

---

[126] Act 3, scene 2, lines 21-25.

## *Oedipus Rex*
## Mythology and the Tragic Hero

The riddle of the Sphinx can never be solved merely by the wit of man.
—C.G. Jung, *Symbols of Transformation.*

# Foreword

In an old parable about the River Jordan, it is said that it flows through the holy land into two seas. One is the beautiful Sea of Galilee, which uses the water it needs while the rest flows on with the Jordan. The other is the lifeless Dead Sea, which takes the water and gives nothing back.

The universal images in this parable are a setting much like the stage on which human beings play out their relation to eternal ideas on the shores of two seas, the sea of life and the sea of death. Each one of us is cast in a living drama as mythic as the flow of the River Jordan.

And we are each blessed with the opportunity to relate our lives to the mythical question of the soul. As Edinger writes (below, page 71), "A knowledge of mythological images is an essential requirement if the ego is to have a conscious relation to the deeper layers of the psyche."

In *"Oedipus Rex:* Mythology and the Tragic Hero," Dr. Edinger reaches back into the flow to the convergence of Greek and Judeo-Christian mythology, and traces it forward to the myths of modern man. He illustrates the individuation process of the tragic hero with examples, in brief anecdotes from Shakespeare, and in depth commentary on the two Oedipus plays of Sophocles.

This essay originally appeared in the very first issue of *Parabola* under the title "The Tragic Hero: An Image of Individuation." In it, Dr. Edinger offers us a four-step psychological interpretation of the "tragic process" in literature:

1) *agone*—in which the ego is defeated;
2) *pathos*—the hero undergoes suffering;
3) *threnos*—lamentation for the defeated hero;
4) *theophany*—rebirth of life at another level, with a reversal of emotion from sorrow to joy.

Indeed, all four plays discussed in this book cycle through the tragic process, each emphasizing one or another of the steps. Taken together, they give an image of the whole alchemical process, from fiery ordeals and suffering to transformation into a sacred object that benefits all.

The first play, *Measure for Measure,* emphasizing *agone,* teaches us about the nature of the Self. The *pathos* of the second, *Romeo and Juliet,* teaches us the meaning of the process of individuation. *Oedipus the King,* the third play, explores *threnos,* illustrating how we ordinary people relate to the archetypal energies of myth, and how we can work our way out of a state of identification with the Self. The fourth play, *Oedipus at Colonus,* takes us beyond the tragic ordeal to rebirth and the symbolic life—to *theophany.*

*The Psyche on Stage* is thus a unifying overview of depth psychology with examples drawn from a great span of time, reaching from Sophocles (450 B.C.E.), through Shakespeare (the 1600's), to its contemporary expressions in psychology. For Dr. Edinger, psychology *is* the modern myth, and no one has expressed it better:

> As the twenty-first century approaches we are witnessing the emergence of a whole new world-view growing out of depth psychology. This new science studies the psyche as an experienceable, objective phenomenon. It takes old data and approaches them in a new way. For instance, mythology, religion and sacred scriptures of all kinds are taken out of their traditional contexts and understood psychologically, . . . seen as the phenomenology of the objective psyche.[127]

I am pleased to introduce you to Dr. Edinger's cogent analysis of *Oedipus the King* and *Oedipus at Colonus.*

*Sheila Dickman Zarrow*

---

[127] *Parabola: The Magazine of Myth and Tradition,* vol. 1, no. 1, p. 11.

**Introduction**

What is mythology, and why should we study it?

To begin with, it fixes in concrete, readily understood forms the universal, archetypal realities which underlie psychic experience, and are especially influential when they are unconscious. A knowledge of mythological images is an essential requirement if the ego is to have a conscious relation to the deeper layers of the psyche. The ego that lacks these categories of understanding will be either confined to the shallow level of subjective meanings, or it will be taken over by the archetypal energies and forced to live them out unconsciously.

So, as I see it, the psychological answer to the question, "Why study mythology?" is that the psyche will otherwise be invisible; only through acquaintance with the incredible diversity of mythological images is the psyche made manifest in its origins, its structure and its transformations.

Mythology, it seems, performs the same service for developing culture and consciousness as does Athena's mirror for Perseus facing Medusa. In fact, this image of Athena's mirror is a very apt symbol for human culture in general, because what culture, and mythology in particular, does is break up the terrifying totality of being into accessible images. The function corresponds to what Shakespeare has to say about the nature of drama in *Hamlet:*

> The purpose of the playing is to hold as 'twere the mirror up to nature, to show virtue her own feature, scorn her own image, and the very age and body of the time his form and pressure.[128]

Myths promote consciousness, providing that the relevant connections with one's own personal life can be made. One must al-

---

[128] Act. 3, scene 2, lines 19-23.

ways ask, "How does this relate to me?" Finding one's own particular myth at any given time can be a very moving experience, for it carries with it a kind of shock of recognition, a sudden realization that that is *I* that's looking back at *me* from the collective mythological images.

Greek mythology is one of the two main roots of the Western psyche, the other being Judeo-Christian mythology. And the Greek myths are therefore our "scriptures" just as much as the Bible is, and should be approached with equal seriousness.

Myths are not stories of remote happenings in the past; they are dramas that are living themselves out repeatedly in our personal lives and in what we see around us here and now. To be aware of this adds a dimension to existence which is usually reserved for the poets. Moses is eternally bringing down the law from Sinai. Jesus is eternally being crucified and resurrected. Likewise, Hercules is eternally performing his labors; Perseus continues to confront Medusa; Theseus forever stalks the Minotaur; Demeter continues to search for Persephone; and all the other myths are always recurring everywhere about us and within us. It may even be that Plato discovered his concept of eternal ideas from contemplating the Greek myths.

It is from this perspective—myth as a mirror of psyche—that I want to treat the theme of the tragic hero.

**The Tragic Hero**

Viewed psychologically, the mythological hero can be defined as a personification of the urge to individuation. He stands midway between the Self and the ego—less than Self but more than ego. The tragic hero is more human than the mythological hero. He has no supernatural powers. He is a limited human being caught like Laocoön in the coils of a transpersonal destiny. He represents the ego gripped by the process of individuation.

The figure of the tragic hero emerged from two outstanding and interrelated instruments of civilization created by the ancient

Greeks—the sacred games and the ritual drama. It is indicative of their psychological similarity that we refer to both games and drama with the same word, "play." These action-forms give human energies a second world in which to function. We are apt to forget the crucial role that games and athletic contests played in civilizing the aggressive energies of early man.

Nietzsche had a profound understanding of this fact, as indicated by the following passage:

> When the victor in a fight among the cities executes the entire male citizenry in accordance with the laws of war, and sells all the women and children into slavery, we see in the sanction of such a law that the Greeks considered it an earnest necessity to let their hatred flow forth fully; in such moments crowded and swollen feeling relieved itself; the tiger leaped out, voluptuous cruelty in his terrible eyes. Why must the Greek sculptor give form again and again to war and combat in innumerable repetitions: distended human bodies, their sinews tense with hatred or with the arrogance of triumph; writhing bodies, wounded; dying bodies, expiring? Why did the whole Greek world exult over the combat scenes of the *Iliad?* I fear that we do not understand these in a sufficiently "Greek" manner; indeed, that we should shudder if we were ever to understand them in Greek.[129]

It is these wild and primitive energies that are contained, channeled, and finally transformed by means of organized games and athletic contests. In the beginning, the games were always dedicated to a god, indicating that the athletes' efforts were being offered up to a transpersonal meaning. Indeed, a transpersonal meaning *is* achieved whenever we succeed in transforming primitive psychic energy by humanizing it.

At such times we are serving the grand enterprise of the evolution of consciousness. I think this is Plato's meaning when he speaks about the need for men to play, in that late work written in his old age, *The Laws:*

---

[129] "Homer's Contest," in Walter Kaufman, ed., *The Portable Nietzsche*, p. 33.

God is the real goal of all beneficent serious endeavor. Man, as we said before, has been constructed as a toy for God, and this is, in fact, the finest thing about him. All of us, then, men and women alike, must fall in with our role and spend life in making our *play* as perfect as possible. We should pass our lives in the playing of games—*certain* games, that is, sacrifice, song, and dance—with the result of ability to gain heaven's grace.[130]

In later thinking the athletic contest, the *agone,* became a paradigm for spiritual development. St. Paul used it for that purpose.[131] Today we can see it as a symbol of the individuation process.

**The Psyche on Stage**

Drama is another type of play which has the capacity to transform primitive psychic energy. Originally drama was the ritual acting-out of a myth. While watching the drama, the spectators became identified with the mythical happening being portrayed, allowing them to participate briefly in the archetypal level of reality.

We know from psychotherapeutic experience that an encounter with the archetypal dimension can have healing and transformative effects. Drama is certainly very important psychologically and has many parallels to dreams. Aristotle described the effect of watching tragedy as a catharsis in which one has the opportunity to release the emotions of pity and fear. The idea is that, just as a possessed person is calmed by the playing of frenzied music, so sad and fearful people are relieved by seeing the emotions which grip them acted out. Thus, the play functions as a mirror which provides an image to objectify the inner affect.

Modern psychology can add another aspect to the significance of tragic drama. The tragic hero depicts the ego facing the challenge of individuation, which is, in part, a tragic process. We define individuation as the ego's progressive awareness of, and relation to, the

---

[130] *The Laws,* p. 292.
[131] 1 Cor. 9:24-27.

Self. But, as Jung has taught us, "the experience of the self is always a defeat for the ego,"[132] and a defeat for the ego is experienced as tragedy.

Gilbert Murray has given us a valuable description of the origin and basic features of the classic tragedy.[133] It is his view that Greek tragedy started as the ritual reenactment of the death and rebirth of the year-spirit (equated with Dionysus), and that this ritual reenactment had four chief features.

First, there is an *agone* or contest in which the protagonist, the representative of the year-spirit, is in contest with darkness or evil. Secondly, there is a *pathos* or passion in which the hero undergoes suffering and defeat. Third is a *threnos* or lamentation for the defeated hero. And fourthly, there is a *theophany,* a rebirth on another level, with a reversal of emotion from sorrow to joy.

This sequence is basically the same as the ritual dramas of Osiris and Christ, each of which displays the characteristic features of the death and rebirth of the year-spirit. In later Greek tragedy the final phase, the *theophany,* almost disappears, perhaps remaining only as a hint. In psychological terms we can say that the sequence of steps which constitute the tragic process involves the overcoming of the ego, the defeat of conscious will, in order that the Self, the final epiphany, may manifest.

The Shakespearean scholar A.C. Bradley speaks of the tragic hero in terms of a fatal flaw. This would correspond to what Jungian psychology knows as the problem of the inferior function.[134] One side of the circle of the personality is always undeveloped and open to the depths. The so-called fatal flaw is thus a typical and characteristic feature of the individual psyche. Bradley also speaks of Shakespeare's tragic heroes as having "a fatal tendency to identify the whole being with one interest, object, passion, or habit

---

[132] *Mysterium Coniunctionis,* CW 14, par. 778.
[133] See *Aeschylus: The Creator of Tragedy.*
[134] See *Psychological Types,* CW 6, pars. 763ff; also Daryl Sharp, *Personality Types: Jung's Model of Typology,* pp. 21ff.

of mind."[135] This, likewise, is a well-known psychological phenomenon in terms of the ego identifying with the superior function; but it leads to the ego's falling victim to its greatest weakness.

Bradley has a description of tragedy that is relevant:

> [In Shakespearean tragedy, man] may be wretched and may be aweful, but he is not small. His lot may be heart-rending and mysterious, but it is not contemptible. The most confirmed of cynics ceases to be a cynic while he reads these plays. And with this greatness of the tragic hero (which is not always confined to him) is connected, secondly, what I venture to describe as the center of the tragic impression. This central feeling is the impression of waste.
>
> With Shakespeare, at any rate, the pity and fear which are stirred by the tragic story seem to unite with, and even to merge in, a profound sense of sadness and mystery, which is due to this impression of waste. "What a piece of work is man," we cry; "so much more beautiful and so much more terrible than we knew! Why should he be so if this beauty and greatness only tortures itself and throws itself away?"
>
> We seem to have before us a type of the mystery of the whole world, the tragic fact which extends far beyond the limits of tragedy. Everywhere, from the crushed rocks beneath our feet to the soul of man, we see power, intelligence, life and glory, which astound us and seem to call for our worship. And everywhere we see them perishing, devouring one another and destroying themselves, often with dreadful pain, as though they came into being for no other end. Tragedy is the typical form of this mystery, because that greatness of soul which it exhibits oppressed, conflicting and destroyed, is the highest existence in our view. It forces the mystery upon us, and it makes us realize so vividly the worth of that which is wasted that we cannot possibly seek comfort in the reflection that all is vanity.[136]

Bradley expresses beautifully how the fourth phase of the ritual drama of the year-spirit, the phase of *theophany,* which no longer

---

[135] *Shakespearean Tragedy: Hamlet, Othello, King Lear, Macbeth,* p. 33.
[136] Ibid., p. 29.

appears in the tragic drama itself, is transferred to the experience of the spectator. In watching the tragedy, the spectator becomes aware of the transpersonal worth of man. The spectator becomes the ground, so to speak, on which the *theophany* is experienced.

This same sequence of four stages—the *agone* or contest, the *pathos* or defeat, the *threnos* or lamentation, and the *theophany*—is found in all important processes of psychological development, and certainly in every psychotherapeutic process that goes at all deep.

At times a given phase may repeat itself. For example, take the first phase, the *agone* or contest. As long as the *agone* ends in success, the process won't go any further. It is short-circuited, so to speak, and the happy victor leaves the scene little knowing that he has missed the main event. But no one experiences success perpetually; sooner or later defeat does come, and that then leads to the possibility of completion of the sequence.

Let us examine now, as an example of the tragic process, two plays of Sophocles, *Oedipus the King* and *Oedipus at Colonus*. They are of particular significance to depth psychology because Oedipus was the first archetype to be discovered, or at least named as such. Freud made the important observation that it can give rise to a complex, the so-called Oedipus complex. Since then we have learned that any archetypal image can manifest itself as a personal complex in the individual psyche.[137]

**Oedipus the King**

*Oedipus the King* begins in the middle of the story and requires an introduction to bring the reader up to date:

Because of an oracle that prophesied that Oedipus would kill his father and marry his mother, Oedipus was abandoned at birth and left for dead. However, unbeknown to his parents, a shepherd rescued the infant and took him to the king of Corinth, who adopted

---

[137] I have personally seen an Orestes complex, an Iphigenia complex, a Hamlet complex, and a Coriolanus complex.

*78 Oedipus Rex*

him and reared him in his own house. About fifteen years before the opening of the play, Oedipus had been told by the oracle at Delphi that he was destined to murder his father and marry his mother. Shocked by this prediction, he determined never to go back to Corinth, whose king and queen he thought were his parents.

Oedipus' wanderings brought him eventually to the city of Thebes where his real father and mother were reigning. However, on the way he brawled with an old man in a carriage over the right of way, and in a fit of temper killed him.

Arriving at Thebes, he finds the city in an uproar because the king, Laius, has gone on a journey and never returned. Also a female monster, the Sphinx, has taken up a position on a rock outside Thebes and is strangling the inhabitants one by one because they are not able to answer her riddle.[138] When Oedipus answers it, the Sphinx throws herself from the rock. In gratitude, the citizens make Oedipus their king and he marries Jocasta, their widowed queen. Of course no one knows that Jocasta is Oepipus' real mother, and that the old man he killed on the road was Laius, his father.

There follow fifteen years of apparent prosperity, but only apparent, because the gods are disgusted by the corruption that exists. Therefore Thebes is struck by a plague. The people, led by their priests and elders, flock around the great and successful Oedipus and ask him to save them. This is where *Oedipus the King* begins.

At the start, Oedipus is in his prime. He signifies the confident ego that thinks it has successfully met life and its problems (represented by the Sphinx) and has nothing more to fear. Concerning Oedipus' overconfidence, Jung writes,

> [The] tragic consequences . . . could easily have been avoided if only Oedipus had been sufficiently intimidated by the frightening appearance of the "terrible" or "devouring" Mother whom the Sphinx personified. . . . Little did he know that the riddle of the

---

[138] The Sphinx asked all who passed: "What goes on four legs in the morning, on two at noon, and three in the evening?"

Sphinx can never be solved merely by the wit of man.

... A factor [i.e., complex] of such magnitude cannot be disposed of by solving a childish riddle. The riddle was, in fact, the trap which the Sphinx laid for the unwary wanderer. Overestimating his intellect in a typically masculine way, Oedipus walked right into it, and all unknowingly committed the crime of incest. The riddle of the Sphinx was *herself*—the terrible mother-imago, which Oedipus would not take as a warning.[139]

Young Oedipus ponders the Sphinx's riddle.
(Detail of an Attic cup, circa 470 B.C.; Vatican Museum, Rome.
Photo: Alinari/Art Resource, New York.)

---

[139] *Symbols of Transformation*, CW 5, pars. 264f.

The play begins with Oedipus in an illusory state of well-being which is suddenly interfered with by the plague that has struck Thebes. He is told to

> ... look upon the city, see the storm
> that batters down this city's prow in waves of blood.
> The crops diseased, disease among the herds,
> The ineffectual womb rotting with its fruit.
> A fever-demon wastes the town
> and decimates with fire, stalking hated
> through the emptied house where Cadmus lived;
> while poverty-stricken night grows fat
> on groans and elegies in Hades Halls.[140]

Here we have the theme of the diseased or barren land, as in the beginning of the Grail legend. The psychological counterpart to this condition is a state of depressed emptiness, a loss of energy, interest and life-meaning. This neurotic condition requires action and Oedipus, the ego, is asked to do something about it:

> So, Oedipus, you most respected king,
> we plead with you to find for us a cure;
> some answer blown from God or—could it be?
> enlightenment from man ...
> Mend the city, make her safe. ...
> Be equal to your stature now.
> If king of men (as king you are),
> then be it of a kingdom manned and not a desert.[141]

Oedipus resolutely sets out to discover what is wrong. There is a distressing symptom that needs attention. This would correspond to the first indication of a psychological problem. One realizes one must act, perhaps by seeking psychotherapy.

In the play, Oedipus sends Creon to consult the oracle at Delphi. The message that comes back is, "Banish the murderer of Laius." In

---

[140] *Oedipus the King*, in Paul Roche, trans., *The Oedipus Plays of Sophocles*, p. 24.
[141] Ibid., pp. 24f.

psychological terms, the unconscious has been consulted, perhaps by attending to one's dreams, and the answer that comes up is to bring the guilty one to justice. In other words, the shadow must be made conscious.

Oedipus readily agrees to this procedure. Little does he know that he himself is the culprit. The evil is his own, but he still naively imagines himself innocent. Oedipus might well be told at this point, "Never send to know for whom the bell tolls; it tolls for thee."[142]

Next, Teiresias the seer is called; that is, the unconscious is consulted again on another level. Replies to Oedipus' questions are gradually forced out of Teiresias. When the incriminating evidence first appears, Oedipus accuses Teiresias and Creon of the crime, just as the first emerging awareness of the shadow leads to its projection. But that won't hold up, and the truth about Oedipus' origin gradually unfolds as he seeks it out. The shepherd is questioned and Oedipus learns that he is Jocasta's child. Jocasta too realizes the dreadful truth and retreats to her chamber. Finally and cataclysmically, the insight bursts upon Oedipus that *he* is the one. Awareness of his identity and his guilt conjoined rushes in on him and he cries:

> Lost! ah lost! At last it's blazing clear.
> Light of my eyes, good bye—my final gaze!
> My birth all sprung revealed from those it never should;
> myself entwined with those I never could;
> and I the killer of those I never would.[143]

Oedipus goes into the palace, sees Jocasta who has hanged herself, and blinds himself with the pins of Jocasta's brooches.

The symbol of blindness has an important role in the plays. It has a paradoxical quality. At the moment Oedipus sees himself as he really is, he blinds himself. Earlier, Teiresias had said to him:

> I'm blind you say. You mock at that! I say
> you see and still are blind—appallingly:

---

[142] John Donne, "Devotions," in Louis Untermeyer, ed. *Great Poems*, p. 98.
[143] *Oedipus the King,* in Roche, trans., *The Oedipus Plays*, p. 70.

> Blind to your origins and to a union
> in your house. Yes, ask yourself, "where are you from?"
> You'd never guess what hate is dormant in your home
> or buried with your dear ones dead;
> or how a mother's and a father's curse
> will one day scourge you with its double thongs
> and whip you staggering from the land.
> It shall be night where now you boast of day.[144]

Oedipus had been blind all along, but when he sees his blindness he blinds himself. When he can see physically, he is blind psychologically; and as he comes to see psychologically, he becomes blind physically. Along with this paradoxical symbolism is the fact that Teiresias the seer is blind, indicating that sight of one kind is deleterious to sight of another kind—as though inner and outer sight work reciprocally.

Let us consider the nature of Oedipus' insight. What he discovered literally was that he had murdered his father and married his mother. These were probably the worst possible crimes of the ancient world. The paternal Logos principle and the maternal Eros principle have both been violated. Simultaneously, Oedipus discovers his identity and his guilt. He experiences for himself the Christian teaching that man is a miserable sinner.

In psychological terms, Oedipus has been overwhelmed by a sudden realization of the shadow. The intensity of his reaction indicates that he has encountered not the personal shadow but the archetypal shadow. The abyss opens before him and he is utterly demoralized. There is a parallel to Oedipus' self-horror in John Bunyan's description of his own self-loathing:

> But my original and inward pollution, that was my plague and my affliction. By reason of that, I was more loathsome in my own eyes than was a toad; and I thought I was in God's eyes too. Sin and corruption, I said, would as naturally bubble out of a fountain. I could

---

[144] Ibid., p. 39.

have changed heart with anybody. I thought none but the Devil himself could equal me of inward wickedness and pollution of mind. . . . I was both a burden and a terror to myself; nor did I ever so know, as now, what it was to be weary of my life, and yet afraid to die. How gladly would I have been anything but myself! Anything but a man! And in any condition but my own.[145]

*Oedipus the King* ends with the total defeat of Oedipus. There is no *theophany*. This is reserved for *Oedipus at Colonus,* which is part two of Oedipus and very similar to part two of Goethe's *Faust.*

## Oedipus at Colonus

As the second play opens, Oedipus has long been banished from Thebes and is wandering from place to place, guided by his daughter. This is significant because the theme of the wanderer is characteristic of one stage of individuation.

Cain was condemned to wander. According to legend, Elijah and the Wandering Jew are both required to wander hopelessly until the Messiah comes. In Gnostic thought, the whole earthly life of man is considered to be a banishment from his heavenly home. Hexagram 56 of the I Ching (next page) is entitled "The Wanderer."

Psychologically, the state of banishment and wandering is a necessary intermediate condition in the process of individuation. One cannot find a durable relation to the inner center, the Self, until one has been deprived of outer containments and identifications.

After long wanderings, Oedipus comes at last to a sacred spot close to Athens. He is now a sage and holy man, a precious sacred entity. His two sons, who are fighting one another for Thebes, both want his approval because an oracle has said that whoever obtains it will be victorious. The oracle has also announced that his tomb will bless the land it's on.

Oedipus has become a sacred object, a living *theophany*. In the following passage he describes the holy power of his tomb:

---

[145] Quoted in William James, *Varieties of Religious Experience,* p. 155.

## 84  Oedipus Rex

Hexagram 56, "The Wanderer."

Come, listen, son of Aegeus,
I'll lay before you now a city's lasting treasure.
There is a place where I must die,
and I myself, unhelped, shall walk before you there.
That place you must not tell to any human being:
not where it lurks, nor where the region lies—
if you would have a shield like a thousand shields,
and a more perpetual pact than spears of allies.
No chart of words shall mark that mystery.
Alone you'll go: alone your memory
shall frame it in that spot.
For not to any persons here
not even to my daughters so beloved
am I allowed to utter it.
You yourself must guard it always.
And when your life is drawing to its close
divulge it to your heir alone
and he in turn to his, and so forever.
This way you'll keep your city safe against the dragon seed,
though many a state attack a peaceful home,
though sure be the help from heaven
(but exceeding slow)
against earth's godless men and men gone mad.
No such fate for you, good son of Aegeus.
But all of this you know without my telling you.
And now to that spot—God signals me.[146]

---

[146] *Oedipus at Colonus,* in Roche, trans., *The Oedipus Plays,* p. 150.

The life of Oedipus, as it is revealed in these two plays, parallels the alchemical process. Like the *prima materia* with which the alchemists began in their efforts to turn base metal into gold, Oedipus is subjected to fiery ordeals and sufferings until he is transformed into a sacred object that benefits all who touch him. Here is the *theophany* that redeems the suffering of the first play.

Taken together, Sophocles' two Oedipus plays reveal explicitly the four stages of tragedy previously mentioned.

The first stage, the *agone* or contest, is represented by Oedipus' encounter with the Sphinx, followed later by the struggle to discover the hidden knowledge that was causing the plague. The second stage, the *pathos* or passion, corresponds to the blinding insight and the ego-defeat which it caused. The *threnos* or lamentation is represented by the chorus which bemoans the downfall of mighty Oedipus followed by his prolonged wanderings. The fourth stage, the *theophany,* comes at the end of *Oedipus at Colonus* when his tomb becomes a sacred sanctuary and a perpetual blessing.

These four stages portray quite precisely the steps in every major increase of consciousness. In each case a suffering, deflating ordeal for the ego must precede the epiphany of the Self. This is necessary because the ego starts out in a state of identification with the Self. It can only realize its separateness and dependent condition by a tragic ordeal which enforces the separation.

Sophocles describes this process in the final lines of *Antigone:*

> Where wisdom is, there happiness will crown
> A piety that nothing will corrode.
> But high and mighty words and ways
> Are flogged to humbleness, till age,
> Beaten to its knees, at last is wise.[147]

---

[147] *Antigone,* in Roche, trans., *The Oedipus Plays,* p. 210.

# Bibliography

Atwood, M.A. *Hermetic Philosophy and Alchemy.* Reprint of 1850 ed. New York: The Julian Press, 1960.

Bald, R.C., ed. *The Pelican Shakespeare: Measure for Measure.* Baltimore: Penguin Books, 1978.

Barnet, Sylvan, ed. *Measure for Measure.* Signet Classic. New York: Penguin Books, 1964.

Baum, Julius, et al. *The Mysteries Papers* (Bollingen Series XXX). Eranos Yearbook. New York: Pantheon Books, 1955.

Bradley, A.C. *Shakespearean Tragedy: Hamlet, Othello, King Lear, Macbeth.* Greenwich, CT: Fawcett Publications Inc., 1965.

Brandon, S.G.F. *The Judgement of the Dead.* New York: Scribners, 1967.

Budge, E.A. Wallis. *The Gods of the Egyptians.* Reprint. New York: Dover, 1969.

Coleridge, Samuel Taylor. *Coleridge's Writings on Shakespeare.* New York: Capricorn Books (Division of G.P. Putnam's Sons), 1959.

Edinger, Edward F. *Anatomy of the Psyche: Alchemical Symbolism in Psychotherapy.* La Salle, IL: Open Court, 1985.

_____. *Ego and Archetype: Individuation and the Religious Function of the Psyche.* Boston: Shambhala Publications, 1992.

_____. *The Mysterium Lectures: A Journey through C.G. Jung's Mysterium Coniunctionis.* Toronto: Inner City Books, 1995.

_____. *The Psyche in Antiquity, Book One: Early Greek Philosophy.* Toronto: Inner City Books, 1999.

_____. *The Psyche in Antiquity, Book Two: Gnosticism and Early Christianity.* Toronto: Inner City Books, 1999.

Freeman, Kathleen. *Ancilla to the Pre-Socratic Philosophers.* Cambridge, MA: Harvard University Press, 1962.

Henderson, Jospeh P. *Cultural Attitudes in Psychological Perspective.* Toronto: Inner City Books, 1984.

Hoffman, Edward. *The Way of Splendor:Jewish Mysticism and Modern Psychology.* Boulder, CO: Shambhala, 1981.

James, William. *Varieties of Religious Experience.* New York: New American Library, 1958.

Jung, C.G. *The Collected Works* (Bollingen Series XX). 20 vols. Trans. R.F.C. Hull. Ed. H. Read, M. Fordham, G. Adler, Wm. McGuire. Princeton: Princeton University Press, 1953-1979.

————. *Memories, Dreams, Reflections.* Ed. Aniela Jaffé. New York: Random House, 1963.

————. *The Visions Seminars.* Zurich: Spring Publications, 1976.

Kaufman, Walter. *The Portable Nietzsche.* New York: Viking Books, 1968.

Leishman, J.B., ed. and trans. *Rilke: Selected Poems.* Harmondsworth, England: Penguin Books, 1964.

Mitchell, Stephen, ed. and trans. *Ahead of All Parting: The Selected Poetry and Prose of Rainer Maria Rilke.* New York: The Modern Library, 1995.

Murray, Gilbert. *Aeschylus: The Creator of Tragedy.* London: Oxford at the Clarendon Press, 1940.

Onions, C.T. *A Shakespeare Glossary.* London: Oxford University Press, 1963.

Plato. *The Laws.* Trans. Trevor J. Saunders. London: Penguin Books, 1975.

Roche, Paul, trans. *The Oedipus Plays of Sophocles.* A Mentor Book. New York: New American Library, 1958.

Rowse, A.L. *William Shakespeare: A Biography.* New York: Harper and Row, 1963.

Shakespeare, William. *Hamlet, Prince of Denmark.* Ed. Willard Farnham. The Pelican Shakespeare. Toronto: Penguin Books, 1957.

————. *Measure for Measure.* Ed. J.W. Lever. Cambridge, MA: Harvard University Press, 1965.

————. *Romeo and Juliet.* Ed. John Dover Wilson, G.I. Duthie. New York: Cambridge University Press, 1959.

Sharp, Daryl. *Personality Types: Jung's Model of Typology.* Toronto: Inner City Books, 1987.

Spurgeon, Caroline F.E. *Shakespeare's Imagery and What It Tells Us.* Cambridge, England: Cambridge University Press, 1975.

Stauffer, Donald. *Shakespeare's World of Images.* New York, 1949.

von Franz, Marie-Louise. *C.G. Jung: His Myth in Our Time.* Toronto: Inner City Books, 1998.

Untermeyer, Louis, ed. *Great Poems.* Pocket Cardinal Edition. Richmond Hill, ON: Simon and Schuster of Canada, 1958.

Watt, Homer; Holzhnect, Karl; Ross, Raymond. *Outlines of Shakespeare's Plays.* New York: Barnes and Noble Books (Division of Harper and Row), 1969.

Zesmer, David M. *Guide to Shakespeare.* New York: Barnes and Noble Outline Series, 1976.

# Index

Page nos. in *italic* refer to illustrations

Adam Kadmon, *35*
affect, 26-27
*agone*, 74-75, 77, 85
alchemy, 33-34, 45, 56, 63, 85
Amor and Psyche, 60
Anaximander, 48
anima, 23, 52n
animus, 27, 52n
Archangel Michael, *30*
archetype(s), 21, 23-25, 38, 47-48, 52-53, 56, 58, 71, 74, 82
Aristotle, 74
art, 65-66
Athena's mirror, 71
authority, delegated, 13

beauty, 51, 65
beheading, 37-38. *See also* dismemberment
Bible/Biblical, 19n, 72. *See also* Books by name
blindness, 81-82
body and spirit, 37-38
Bradley, A.C.: *Shakespearean Tragedy*, 75-76
Bunyan, John, 82

*calcinatio*, 34
Christ/Christian, 19, 29, 33, 35-36, 40, 75, 82
Clement, 36
Coleridge, Samuel Taylor, on *Measure for Measure*, 15

complex, 77
*coniunctio*, 23-25, 37-39, 47, 53, 56, 58-59
  lesser and greater, 45
consciousness, 36, 48, 65-66, 71, 73
  Jung on, 13-14
  moral, 31

death, 63
  and love, 52, 59, 65
  marriage to, 60
  and rebirth, 75
decapitation, 37-38
delegated authority, 13
depression, 80
dismemberment, 52-53, 55-56. *See also* beheading
Divine Wisdom, 33, 39
dove, *50*
drama, 74
  Greek, 73
  Shakespeare on, 71

Ecclesiasticus, Book of, 39
ego, 25, 31, 3, 487, 58, 59, 71, 76
  in *Oedipus the King*, 78, 80
  in *Romeo and Juliet*, 46
  and Self, 13-14, 63, 72, 74-75
  in *Measure for Measure*, 17-40
  in *Romeo and Juliet*, 52
  in *Oedipus the King* and

*Oedipus at Colonus*, 85
and unconscious, 33
enantiodromia, 27, 39
Eros, 39, 49, 82
envy, 32
fall, 23
fanatic/fanaticism, 25
Freud, Sigmund, 77
function, inferior/superior, 75-76

games, sacred, 73
  Plato on, 74
Genesis (Book of), 48
"glassy essence," 34
God/God-image, 19, 34-35, 40
  paradoxical, 15, 35, 40
  transformation of, 41
Goddess of Justice, 27, *28*
grace, 29
Greek, culture, 73
  mythology, 72
  tragedy, 75
gunpowder, 58

*Hamlet*, 14, 71
Henderson, Joseph, 46
hero, tragic, 72-

identification/identity, 17-18, 52-54, 56, 74, 76, 83, 85
*imago Dei*, 32
imbalance, 22
individuation, 23, 25, 45, 62, 72, 74, 83
inferior, 25
  function, 75
inflation, 23, 32, 58

Israel, 19, 2, 391
Job, Book of, 21
Jordan River, 69
Jung, C.G./Jungian, 15, 27, 36
  *Aion*, 34-35, 41
  "Answer to Job," 32
  on archetype(s), 21n
  on beheading, 38
  *C.G. Jung Letters*, 40
  on *coniunctio*, 37-38
  on consciousness, 13-14
  on dismemberment, 52-53, 56
  on ego and Self, 13-14, 75
  on God-image, 40-41
  on love, 49, 62
  *Memories, Dreams, Reflections*, 49
  *Mysterium Coniunctionis*, 37-38, 48-49, 56, 75
  on Oedipus, 78-79
  on opposites, 48-49
  on paradoxical Self-image, 37
  on power, 62
  psychology, 13
  "The Psychology of the Transference," 47, 62, 63
  on the Self, 34, 75
  *Symbols of Transformation*, 79
  "Transformation Symbolism in the Mass," 13-14
  *Two Essays on Analytical Psychology*, 33, 62
  on the unconscious, 33
  *The Visions Seminars*, vol. 1, 52-53
Judgment, Last, 29
Justice, Goddess of, 27, *28*

Kabbala, 35
*King Lear,* 14
king, and queen, *50, 61*
 slaying of, *57*
Knight, G.Wilson: *"Measure for Measure* and the Gospels," 19

Last Judgment (Egyptian), *29*
Law, and Mercy, 23-25
lesser and greater, 51
 *coniunctio,* 45
light, 65-66
Logos, 82
love, 49, 51, 56
 and death, 52, 65
 and power, 62-63

*Macbeth,* 15
*mana,* 51
Marcion, 35
marriage, to death, 60
Matthew, Book of, 19, 33, 40
meaning, 73
meaninglessness, 25
*Measure for Measure,* 13-42
 critical comments on, 14-15
 ego and Self in, 17-40
 "glassy essence," 34
 Law and Mercy in, 23-25
 summary, 15-16
Melville, Herman: *Billy Budd,* 25
Mercy, Law and, 23-25
Michael, Archangel, *30*
mirror of the psyche, 72
moral consciousness, 31
Moses, 20

Murray, Gilbert: *Aeschylus: The Creator of Tragedy,* 75
myth/mythology, 71, 74
 as mirror of the psyche, 72
 personal, 72

New Testament, 40
Nietzsche, Friedrich: "Homer's Contest," 73
*numinosum,* 49

Oedipus, 72-85. *See also under* Sophocles
opposite(s), 22-25, 27, 34, 36-38, 40, 48, 55-56, 63
 united/union of, 62
 warring, 54
original wholeness, 18
Osiris, 75
*Othello,* 14

paradoxical God-image, 15, 35, 40
*pathos,* 75, 77, 85
Persephone, 60
Philosophers' Stone, 33
Plato, 72,
 *The Laws,* 73-74
possession, 27
power, animus, 27
 and love, 62-63
 problem, 21
principle(s), 25, 27
projection, 23, 25, 52, 81
Proverbs, Book of, 33
Psyche, and Amor, 60
psychology, depth, 70
 Jungian, 13

rebirth, 63, *64*, 75
religious attitude, 29
Rilke, Rainer Maria: *Duino Elegies*, 49
*Romeo and Juliet*, 45-66
   ego and Self in, 52
*Rosarium philosophorum*, 47, 49, 60, 63, *64*
Rowse, A.L.: *William Shakespeare: A Biography*, 14, 38

*Sapientia Dei*, 33
Satan, 35
Sefirotic Tree, *35*
Self, 15, 24, 29, 31, 39, 52, 83
   and affect, 27
   on drama, 71
   and ego, 13-14, 63, 72, 74-75
      in *Measure for Measure*, 17-40
      in *Romeo and Juliet*, 52
      in Sophocles: *Oedipus the King* and *Oedipus at Colonus*, 85
   Jung on, 34, 75
   Shakespeare on, 19-20
*separatio*, 2, 487
shadow, 23, 55, 81-82
Shakespeare, William, 14-15, 38-40. *See also* plays by name
   on beauty, in *Romeo and Juliet*, 65
   on the Self, 19-20
sin, 25, 48
Sophocles, 69
   *Antigone*, 25, 85
   *Oedipus at Colonus*, 77, 83-85

   *Oedipus the King*, 77-83
      summary, 77-78, 80
soul, *29, 30*
Sphinx, *79*
spirit, and body, 37-38
St. Paul, 74
Stauffer, Donald: *Shakespeare's World of Images*, 65

Tarot, 27, *28*
*theophany*, 75-77, 83, 85
*threnos*, 75, 77, 85
tragedy, 74-77
tragic, hero, 72-
   process, 69-70, 75-77, 85
transference, 25
transformation/transformative, 74
transpersonal, 51, 56, 58, 63, 71, 73
Tree, Sefirotic, *35*
truth, 65

unacknowledged opposite, 26
unconscious, 25-26, 31, 36, 71, 81
   and ego, 33
*unio mentalis*, 37-38
union of opposites, 25, 34, 47

virtue, 29

wanderer, 83
warring opposites, 54
wholeness, 21, 55-56
   original, 17-18
Wisdom, Divine, 33, 39

Yahweh, 19-21, 36, 39

# Also by Edward F. Edinger in this series

**EGO AND SELF: The Old Testament Prophets**
ISBN 0-919123-91-0. (2000) 160 pp. **10 illustrations** $16

**THE PSYCHE IN ANTIQUITY**
Book 1: Early Greek Philosophy. ISBN 0-919123-86-4. (1999) 128 pp. $16
Book 2: Gnosticism and Early Christianity. ISBN 0-919123-87-2. (1999) 160 pp. $16

**THE AION LECTURES: Exploring the Self in Jung's** *Aion*
ISBN 0-919123-72-4. (1996) 208 pp. **30 illustrations** $18

**MELVILLE'S MOBY-DICK: An American Nekyia**
ISBN 0-919123-70-8. (1995) 160 pp. $16

**THE MYSTERIUM LECTURES**
A Journey Through Jung's *Mysterium Coniunctionis*
ISBN 0-919123-66-X. (1995) 352 pp. **90 illustrations** $25

**THE MYSTERY OF THE CONIUNCTIO**
Alchemical Image of Individuation
ISBN 0-919123-67-8. (1994) 112 pp. **48 illustrations** $16

**TRANSFORMATION OF THE GOD-IMAGE**
An Elucidation of Jung's *Answer to Job*
ISBN 0-919123-55-4. (1992) 144 pp. $16

**GOETHE'S FAUST: Notes for a Jungian Commentary**
ISBN 0-919123-44-9. (1990) 112 pp. $16

**THE CHRISTIAN ARCHETYPE**
A Jungian Commentary on the Life of Christ
ISBN 0-919123-27-9. (1987) 144 pp. **34 illustrations** $16

**THE BIBLE AND THE PSYCHE**
Individuation Symbolism in the Old Testament
ISBN 0-919123-23-6. (1986) 176 pp. $18

**ENCOUNTER WITH THE SELF**
A Jungian Commentary on William Blake's *Illustrations of the Book of Job*
ISBN 0-919123-21-X. (1986) 80 pp. **22 illustrations** $15

**THE CREATION OF CONSCIOUSNESS**
Jung's Myth for Modern Man
ISBN 0-919123-13-9. (1984) 128 pp. **10 illustrations** $16

# Studies in Jungian Psychology by Jungian Analysts

Quality Paperbacks

*Prices and payment in $US (except in Canada, $Cdn)*

**The Secret Raven: Conflict and Transformation**
Daryl Sharp (Toronto). ISBN 0-919123-00-7. 128 pp. $16

**The Psychological Meaning of Redemption Motifs in Fairy Tales**
Marie-Louise von Franz (Zürich). ISBN 0-919123-01-5. 128 pp. $16

**Alchemy: An Introduction to the Symbolism and the Psychology**
Marie-Louise von Franz (Zürich). ISBN 0-919123-04-X. 288 pp. $20

**Descent to the Goddess: A Way of Initiation for Women**
Sylvia Brinton Perera (New York). ISBN 0-919123-05-8. 112 pp. $16

**Addiction to Perfection: The Still Unravished Bride**
Marion Woodman (Toronto). ISBN 0-919123-11-2. 208 pp. $18pb/$25hc

**Jungian Dream Interpretation: A Handbook of Theory and Practice**
James A. Hall, M.D. (Dallas). ISBN 0-919123-12-0. 128 pp. $16

**The Creation of Consciousness: Jung's Myth for Modern Man**
Edward F. Edinger (Los Angeles). ISBN 0-919123-13-9. 128 pp. $16

**The Analytic Encounter: Transference and Human Relationship**
Mario Jacoby (Zürich). ISBN 0-919123-14-7. 128 pp. $16

**Change of Life: Dreams and the Menopause**
Ann Mankowitz (Ireland). ISBN 0-919123-15-5. 128 pp. $16

**The Illness That We Are: A Jungian Critique of Christianity**
John P. Dourley (Ottawa). ISBN 0-919123-16-3. 128 pp. $16

**Cultural Attitudes in Psychological Perspective**
Joseph L. Henderson, M.D. (San Francisco). ISBN 0-919123-18-X. 128 pp. $16

**The Vertical Labyrinth: Individuation in Jungian Psychology**
Aldo Carotenuto (Rome). ISBN 0-919123-19-8. 144 pp. $16

**The Pregnant Virgin: A Process of Psychological Transformation**
Marion Woodman (Toronto). ISBN 0-919123-20-1. 208 pp. $18pb/$25hc

**Encounter with the Self: William Blake's *Illustrations of the Book of Job***
Edward F. Edinger (Los Angeles). ISBN 0-919123-21-X. 80 pp. $15

**The Scapegoat Complex: Toward a Mythology of Shadow and Guilt**
Sylvia Brinton Perera (New York). ISBN 0-919123-22-8. 128 pp. $16

**The Jungian Experience: Analysis and Individuation**
James A. Hall, M.D. (Dallas). ISBN 0-919123-25-2. 176 pp. $18

**Phallos: Sacred Image of the Masculine**
Eugene Monick (Scranton, PA). ISBN 0-919123-26-0. 144 pp. $16

**Touching: Body Therapy and Depth Psychology**
Deldon Anne McNeely (Lynchburg, VA). ISBN 0-919123-29-5. 128 pp. $16

**Personality Types: Jung's Model of Typology**
Daryl Sharp (Toronto). ISBN 0-919123-30-9. 128 pp. $16

**The Sacred Prostitute: Eternal Aspect of the Feminine**
Nancy Qualls-Corbett (Birmingham). ISBN 0-919123-31-7. 176 pp. $18

**When the Spirits Come Back**
Janet O. Dallett (Seal Harbor, WA). ISBN 0-919123-32-5. 160 pp. $16

**The Mother: Archetypal Image in Fairy Tales**
Sibylle Birkhäuser-Oeri (Zürich). ISBN 0-919123-33-3. 176 pp. $18

**The Survival Papers: Anatomy of a Midlife Crisis**
Daryl Sharp (Toronto). ISBN 0-919123-34-1. 160 pp. $16

**The Cassandra Complex: Living with Disbelief**
Laurie Layton Schapira (New York). ISBN 0-919123-35-X. 160 pp. $16

**Acrobats of the Gods: Dance and Transformation**
Joan Dexter Blackmer (Wilmot Flat, NH). ISBN 0-919123-38-4. 128 pp. $16

**Eros and Pathos: Shades of Love and Suffering**
Aldo Carotenuto (Rome). ISBN 0-919123-39-2. 160 pp. $16

**The Ravaged Bridegroom: Masculinity in Women**
Marion Woodman (Toronto). ISBN 0-919123-42-2. 224 pp. $20

**Liberating the Heart: Spirituality and Jungian Psychology**
Lawrence W. Jaffe (Berkeley). ISBN 0-919123-43-0. 176 pp. $18

**The Dream Story**
Donald Broadribb (Baker's Hill, Australia). ISBN 0-919123-45-7. 256 pp. $20

**The Rainbow Serpent: Bridge to Consciousness**
Robert L. Gardner (Toronto). ISBN 0-919123-46-5. 128 pp. $16

**Circle of Care: Clinical Issues in Jungian Therapy**
Warren Steinberg (New York). ISBN 0-919123-47-3. 160 pp. $16

**Jung Lexicon: A Primer of Terms & Concepts**
Daryl Sharp (Toronto). ISBN 0-919123-48-1. 160 pp. $16

**Body and Soul: The Other Side of Illness**
Albert Kreinheder (Los Angeles). ISBN 0-919123-49-X. 112 pp. $16

**The Secret Lore of Gardening: Patterns of Male Intimacy**
Graham Jackson (Toronto). ISBN 0-919123-53-8. 160 pp. $16

**Getting To Know You: The Inside Out of Relationship**
Daryl Sharp (Toronto). ISBN 0-919123-56-2. 128 pp. $16

**Conscious Femininity: Interviews with Marion Woodman**
Introduction by Marion Woodman (Toronto). ISBN 0-919123-59-7. 160 pp. $16

**The Middle Passage: From Misery to Meaning in Midlife**
James Hollis (Houston). ISBN 0-919123-60-0. 128 pp. $16

**Chicken Little: The Inside Story** *(A Jungian Romance)*
Daryl Sharp (Toronto). ISBN 0-919123-62-7. 128 pp. $16

**Coming To Age: The Croning Years and Late-Life Transformation**
Jane R. Prétat (Providence, RI). ISBN 0-919123-63-5. 144 pp. $16

**Under Saturn's Shadow: The Wounding and Healing of Men**
James Hollis (Houston). ISBN 0-919123-64-3. 144 pp. $16

*Discounts:* any 3-5 books, 10%; 6-9 books, 20%; 10 or more, 25%
Add Postage/Handling: 1-2 books, $3; 3-4 books, $5; 5-9 books, $10; 10 or more, free

Write or phone for free Catalogue of **over 90 titles** and **Jung at Heart** newsletter

**INNER CITY BOOKS, Box 1271, Station Q, Toronto, ON M4T 2P4, Canada**
Tel. 416- 927-0355   /   Fax 416-924-1814   /   E-mail info@innercitybooks.net